# MEN AT THE TOP

# MEN

## AT THE

# TOP

## OSBORN ELLIOTT

H|B

## HARPER & BROTHERS
## NEW YORK

MEN AT THE TOP
*Copyright © 1959*
*by Osborn Elliott*

*Printed in the*
*United States*
*of America*

*All rights in this*
*book are reserved.*
*No part of the*
*book may be used*
*or reproduced*
*in any manner*
*whatsoever without*
*written permission*
*except in the*
*case of brief*
*quotations embodied*
*in critical articles*
*and reviews.*
*For information*
*address*
*Harper & Brothers*
*49 East 33rd Street,*
*New York 16, N. Y.*

L-I

*Library of Congress*
*catalog card number:*
*59-10579*

*To Deirdre*

# CONTENTS

INTRODUCTION    ix

**1.**
THE CHALLENGE    **3**

**2.**
FOUR-WHEEL DRIVE    **21**

**3.**
THE CHANGE: CHESS VS. CHECKERS    **36**

**4.**
UP FROM SOMETHING    **53**

**5.**
THE KID IN THE BLACK VELVET SUIT    **66**

**6.**
THE PRIDE OF THE PRO    **80**

**7.**
THE EXECUTIVE FLESH MARKET    **96**

**8.**
MEN AT WORK    **112**

**9.**
HOME WAS NEVER LIKE THIS    **130**

**10.**
THE CIVIC LIFE    **146**

**11.**
CLUB MEN ALL    **159**

**12.**
THE DIRECTOR: THEORY AND FACT    **172**

# CONTENTS

**13.**
MR. EXECUTIVE GOES TO WASHINGTON    **185**

**14.**
POLITICS: TOGETHER WE STAND?    **202**

**15.**
LOOKING FOR THE ANSWERS    **222**

INDEX    **237**

# INTRODUCTION

H. J. HEINZ II, the Pittsburgh food producer, strode to the door of his immaculate office. "Why write a book about the American executive?" he asked. "Why not leave the poor guy alone? Hasn't he been over-dissected and overanalyzed? After all, anyone can be made to look foolish if he's held close enough to the light for long enough. I'm against the whole project. Who cares?"

This rather unsettling incident took place at the beginning of a ten-city tour of the U.S. which I made in the fall of 1958 to gather material for this book, and for his searching questions I herewith tender my thanks to Mr. Heinz. Apparently, my answers were satisfactory, for in the interview that followed he co-operated as fully as did any of the other two-hundred-odd top businessmen who gave so freely of their time and ideas in the preparation of this book.

The book springs from the conviction that the chief executives of American business and industry, so recently emerged as leaders of the nation, have long been misrepresented, and continue to be so, both by their paid eulogizers and by their professional critics. This is not a scientific book, nor is it statistical, nor even inclusive. I have not set out to prove anything. I did not start from a conviction that these men at the top are all crusaders for the true and good in life, nor that they all sit in their executive suites with knives at the ready beneath their waistcoats, nor that they have been stultified by the rigors of the organization life. I have attempted to play the role of reporter, and if by reporting fairly I have contributed some new information and a greater measure of insight into U.S. business and its leaders, I will have accomplished what I set out to do.

My sample was drawn chiefly from among the top men in the nation's hundred largest corporations, and to this group I added others from smaller firms because of special interest or because they helped illustrate new trends in management. The first step in my research was to send out nearly three hundred questionnaires to executives all over the country. The four-page questionnaire included more than sixty questions; there were answers from eighty men in all, ranging from hastily scribbled notes (in answer to one question concerning executives' wives, a Midwesterner penciled: "Never mind the wife—she don't count—talks too much") to long and thoughtful letters—some of them five thousand words and more—from such men as the president of General Electric, the chairman of the Morgan Guaranty Bank, and the former boss of Chrysler. In almost every case the answers were given with no restrictions on their use.

My trip around the country took me from Richard K. Mellon in Pittsburgh to Sam Goldwyn in Hollywood, from the leading banker (Fred Florence) and the leading retailer (Stanley Marcus) in Dallas to the heads of General Motors, C.B.S., A.T.&T., I.B.M. and many other companies in New York, from the top men of Montgomery Ward and Inland Steel in Chicago to the leaders of the aircraft industry on the West Coast and to the biggest retailer in the Southeast (the boss of Rich's department store in Atlanta). By the time my research associate, Rod Gander, and I were finished, we had talked to the world's largest producers and sellers of chemicals, steel, shoes, aircraft, oil, clothing, automobiles, insurance, electronic equipment and many other goods and services.

To all these men go my thanks—and my apologies to those who, by inadvertence, have not been included in the book.

Through all the months of research, Rod Gander proved himself a tireless, strong and able reporter with a keen mastery of the interviewing art and a sure eye for detail. He is a relentless pursuer of fact.

I am also indebted to Malcolm Muir, the editor-in-chief of *Newsweek*, who not only made it possible for me to undertake this project, but also gave invaluable guidance, and to editor John Denson and executive editor Malcolm Muir, Jr., whose encouragement was always there when needed, as it often was.

Valuable help came from many other associates at *Newsweek*. I am particularly grateful to the following members of the staff for all they did: James C. Jones, Hobart Rowen, William A. Emerson, Jr., Harry Homewood, Betty Voigt, William Flynn, Leon Volkov, John McManaman, and Robert S. Saalfield, Jr. I also appreciate the help of Irwin Goodwin of Science Research Associates. For their able secretarial assistance I thank Judith Spiegelman, Denise Pack, Joan McHale and Nitsa Spanos.

Cass Canfield, Jr., has been an understanding, perceptive and imaginative friend and editor throughout, and for his warmth and judgment I am especially grateful.

It is customary, in an introduction of this sort, for the author to end by thanking his family for their forbearance, cheerfulness, understanding, tender loving care and general saintliness during his hours, days, weeks and months of lonely travail. I thank my own family for all this—and my wife, in particular, for this and much more. She undertook to attack a mountain of raw research and to mine it for every useful nugget of fact and opinion, and then to sort it and refine it. More than that, she was a keen and constructive critic as the book progressed, and her ideas were both stimulating and invaluable. Only she will ever know how hard she worked. But only I will ever know how impossible it would have been to write this book without her.

OSBORN ELLIOTT

# 1.

# THE

# CHALLENGE

THE MAN WITH THE black mustache took a final sip of water, brushed his mouth with a napkin, and rose from the lunch table. There to hear this dark-visaged visitor, in a dining room at Ford Motor Co.'s ultramodern office building in Detroit, sat 13 of his staunchest adversaries. The speaker was a Communist, and his listeners included some of capitalism's most ardent advocates. There was young Henry Ford himself, whose very name for years had conjured up visions of beneficent capitalism in every corner of the world. Then there was Ernest Breech, the professional manager whom Ford had picked to rescue his family company from the brink of financial disaster after World War II. There was General Motors' new chairman, Frederic G. Donner, the financial wizard and $375,000-a-year boss of the biggest manufacturing company in the world; and there were the top men of a giant business-machines company (Burroughs), a giant private utility (Detroit Edison), a giant department store (J. L. Hudson of Detroit).

These No. 1 men of American business all had come to lunch, that January day in 1959, to have a look at the

No. 2 Red of Soviet Russia. And Anastas I. Mikoyan, until then the topmost Communist ever to visit the U.S., chose the occasion to restate the twentieth-century's historic challenge. Mikoyan's words were Russian ("Davaitye sarevnovatsya") but he spoke a language these men could understand: "Let's compete."

This challenge was no mere invitation to cross swords on the battlefield of productivity; it was not just a taunt to build better satellites, bigger bridges, dams and steel mills in the far corners of the world. All these were part of it, of course—but only part. The challenge, put so simply by Mikoyan, struck at the very core of American life and belief. And the men who sat before Mikoyan, along with their brethren who head up the rest of U.S. industry, are the men, above all, who must respond. Not only do they and their companies provide the nation's industrial and military might; from them, too, come the drive, the inspiration, the direction—and the money—for everything from symphony orchestras to scientific laboratories, and for the many other things that go to make America's nonmaterial wealth as well.

From their ranks come many of the people who run the government at local, state and national levels; indeed, as a group these men are far more powerful than any governmental body. Governments may come and go, but these men at the top have a continuity that is unique.

Through the funds and foundations they control, the library and hospital boards they sit on, the charity drives they run, the academic institutions they support, their influence is vast. They account, for example, for more than half the membership of Harvard College's Board of Overseers, which includes a former president of United

**4**

Fruit, a railroader, an insurance man, the biggest maker of men's clothing in the world (Meyer Kestnbaum of Hart Schaffner & Marx), and Dallas retailer Stanley Marcus, who has made the name of an American city synonymous with his store. Half of the fourteen trustees of the $2 billion Ford Foundation were drawn from business (one of them used to be chairman of Standard Oil of New Jersey); and half of the trustees of New York's Metropolitan Museum of Art came to that board from the marts of trade—two of them from the biggest corporation of them all, American Telephone & Telegraph.

Who are these men? Where do they come from? How do they work and live? What do they think about the world? What makes them tick? And what are their chances of responding with the necessary vision, force and imagination to the mortal challenge that has been thrust upon them—and upon all Americans—from abroad?

The stereotypes produced by the novelists, by the writers for Broadway, television and Hollywood, by the politicians and by the commentators on the business scene, are as familiar as they are inaccurate. There is, to begin with, the paunchy, cigar-chomping tycoon, stuffed behind his capacious desk, with four telephones and four secretaries all ajangle within arm's reach. This is the fellow who, in song and story, spends a good part of his time toasting the shade of Bob Taft and high tariffs at the Union League Club by day, and who, by night, gives the "Democrat" party what-for at the local Economic Club. Then there is the ulcerous Handsome Dan in the gray flannel suit, handcuffed to his brief case, commuter timetable, lunchtime martinis and gooseneck putter (he always golfs, so one legend goes, with his business competitors—a fine opportunity for surreptitious price fixing, carefully planned eye gouging and other crimes of collusion).

There are stereotypes to fit almost any plot: the immigrant lad who shined so many Wall Street shoes that he knew exactly what to do—buy up the biggest shoe company in the world; the king of finance who has a paddle tennis court in his private ocean liner, and a playmate in every port; the piratical raider whose bold and cut-throat tactics are fearfully awaited as he musters his crew for the next proxy fight.

And now we are even beginning to hear of a sympathetic business type—or at least a character who fairly groans for sympathy. This is the machine man who, we are told, is lost in the bowels of the giant business organization, his imagination stifled, his drive inhibited, but his nose clean.

Finally, set in counterpoint to all these variations on a theme, is the press agent's saintly captain of industry—the executive who knows every one of his 23,375 employees by his first name, who likes nothing better than a chance to mingle at the annual company outing, who has just left behind him the petty worries of the balance sheet and now (since his new public relations man went to work) is trying his wings as a Business Statesman. "Some of these men come to me," New York publicist Benjamin Sonnenberg once said, "to have a bridge built. I build cantilever extensions into posterity."

But the stereotype artists these days are troubled by an occupational hazard: Every time they seem to be developing a clear picture, the plate shatters.

What is the image of an automobile tycoon? For a while, it was the rough and ready, up-from-the-bench mechanic; then the blunt-speaking engineer; and then came the smiling salesman of consuming drive, quick decision and public charm.

But today? The most spectacular automan now on the scene is a former Mormon missionary. President George Romney of American Motors, who led the way back to smaller, cheaper cars, recently has been preaching another form of heresy (for any automan) with similar missionary zeal: He says General Motors ought to be broken up, to make the automobile business more competitive.

About the last man to agree with Romney would be General Motors' own boss, Frederic Donner. But chairman Donner is hardly the picture of an avaricious monopolist —nor does he, for that matter, resemble any of his automotive forebears. He is no glad-handing salesman (in fact, he has never sold a car in his life); he is no devil-take-the-hindmost production man (it would be hard to imagine him changing a tire); nor is he handy with many tools of the engineer's trade (he shuns the slide rule because, he says, "it's too slow"). Donner is a taciturn and thoughtful financial man who has spent most of his life poring over work sheets of statistics and astonishing his colleagues with his photographic memory for figures. "No Hollywood casting director would have picked me for the role of General Motors chief," he says of himself. "I didn't particularly want this job, and I don't feel a damn bit different now than I did before." In fact, when Donner was offered the G.M. chairmanship by a committee of directors, he said: "Give me a week to think it over." After all, he explained later, "this isn't a job in which you can say, 'Peace, it's wonderful.'" Donner finally decided to take it. "My wife told me she couldn't stand the idea of living the next ten years with me regretting that I had turned it down."

No industry is more basic than steel, and few types are more firmly fixed in the public mind than the steel tycoon. What kind of man is today's steel baron? Is he a horny-handed graduate of the blast furnace, or a latter-day Andrew Carnegie, lashing his underlings to ever greater efforts with his scathing sarcasm? Not at all. Roger Blough, the quiet man in horn-rimmed glasses who currently guides the fortunes of U.S. Steel, comes from Mennonite stock. He was raised on a truck farm in Pennsylvania, and expected to be a farmer himself. Blough went on from the one-room local school to college only because his teacher insisted; he worked as a lawyer for eleven years before joining Big Steel. Instead of administering Carnegie-style tongue lashings to his employees, Blough has been known to call up an assistant early in the morning and read him the newspapers over the phone until the man is sufficiently wide awake to talk business.

What about the traditionally cold and stodgy banker?

It is 8:30 on a winter Sunday morning in Atlanta, Georgia. The streets are quiet—quiet, that is, save for the well-muffled whir of a shiny tan Rolls Royce as it glides down Peachtree Street. The man at the wheel is a short, balding fellow in his mid-forties; he has a wad of gum in one side of his mouth, a floppy tweed hat jammed on his head, white Indian moccasins on his feet, and a shabby khaki shirt and trousers in between. He turns a corner and draws up outside the stately building that houses the headquarters of the Citizens & Southern National Bank. Out he hops, dragging a fat brief case behind him. He goes to a side door, lets himself in with a key, and marches across the marble banking floor to an office in the corner. The room is the very model of a modern bank president's place of business—paneled oak walls, mahogany desk, green leather furniture. But on the wooden door, the sign that should say PRESIDENT proclaims quite another message. In neat gold letters, it announces: IT'S A WONDERFUL WORLD. The man in khaki plumps into a chair, cocks his moccasined feet on the desk and begins to dictate into a machine. Mills B. Lane, president of the biggest bank in the Southeast, has arrived for a little Sunday work.

At a time when other bankers in the country have been campaigning to "humanize" themselves in the public eye, Mills Lane doesn't even have to try. He is so human that fellow bankers, he says with an explosive cackle, "think I'm terrible." Lane reflects for a minute, and drawls: "So do I, sometimes." He calls himself a promoter, not a banker, but his competitors have learned that he is both— and a financial genius, too. By his unorthodox aggressiveness, Lane built Citizens & Southern's assets up from $307 million to $636 million in ten years, soaring past every competitor within a range of 400 miles.

A few years ago, Lane was in a race with a competitor to open a new branch bank in an outlying Atlanta neighborhood. It seemed the competition was likely to win, getting its branch built and open first, and thus snaring all the new customers. Lane vowed not to lose the race. He erected a log cabin next to the building site and opened up for business weeks before the competition could complete its branch. "We called it the Frontier Bank," Lane recalls proudly. "We sent out every clerk and officer to spread the word. They rang five thousand doorbells in one day for the opening blitz and the customers came pouring in."

Another time, Lane had the wild and woolly notion that it would be a good thing for the economy of Georgia —and for his bank—to stimulate a lively sheep-raising business in the state. He picked fourteen farmers from all over Georgia and gave them each a flock of twenty-five hundred animals for the experiment. It worked so well that the sheep population of the state soon sextupled. To celebrate, Lane herded a flock of sheep into his Atlanta headquarters, and more than one regular depositor had to pitch in that day as an emergency shepherd.

"I don't work," Lane says, slapping his khaki breeches. "I just have fun." What has he learned in his twenty-five years as a banker? He points to the golden sign on his office door. "That's what I've learned, son. It's a wonderful world!"

Legend would have it that the lawyer is as stodgy as the banker. But is the lawyer-turned-businessman just an encyclopedia of the securities and antitrust laws, forever accumulating reasons for *not* moving in new and imaginative directions? John Connor, the young president of Merck & Co., got his start as a government lawyer. But he approaches his present job more as a salesman.

"Running a large international business," he says, "is a humbling experience. At every turn the chief executive must be prepared to persuade people that his point of view must prevail. He shouldn't make up his own mind, of course, until he's talked the problem over with the experts; then he's got to see to it that others are persuaded, because if a plan doesn't have their active co-operation they can sabotage it. The top executive also has to discuss a new plan at the board level and get agreement. And after the final decision is made, he's got to continue to be persuasive because the die-hards have to be persuaded that they contributed to the thinking, even though they may have opposed the whole idea. After all, you don't fire people for sticking to a point of view."

And what of the scientist-turned-businessman? Is he interested only in the latest bit of wizardry from the electronics lab?

In a magnificent new office building at Santa Monica, California, Drs. Simon Ramo and Dean Wooldridge (whose company helped develop the Atlas, Titan and Thor missiles), are entertaining a visitor at lunch. They serve martinis from a glass shaker with a metal core containing ice. "That," says Ramo in his best laboratory jargon, "is to minimize the dilution factor."

For two hours Ramo and Wooldridge talk with their visitor, ranging over the entire span of human affairs. They talk of music (Ramo plays the organ as a hobby, Wooldridge the violin), of education (Ramo has given several hundred lectures at Cal. Tech. in recent years, and has helped U.C.L.A. launch a number of extension courses), and of the role of the scientist in an industrial society—particularly the scientist whose life is dedicated to developing new and better weapons of destruction. "My interest in science is ideological to some extent," says Ramo; "the pursuit of truth is appealing. Of course, I'd be happier if we didn't have to guarantee peace by making weapons of war. But if we're going to have this kind of a world, I'm happy to provide the deterrents. If I were in medicine, I'd rather be working on a cancer cure than taking out tonsils."

The good life supposedly enjoyed by the men at the top has also been the subject of countless clichés and romantic generalizations. The visions of Cadillacs and country clubs, the long lunch at "21," the fat expense account, the ocean-going yacht, the executive washroom, the reserved parking space outside the factory door, the three-window office —all these are presumably the hallmarks of success.

But when has a person really arrived in this best of all possible worlds? One columnist has suggested that a man obviously has it made if he goes to lunch at one o'clock instead of noon; if he goes to work at 9:30 instead of 9, and leaves at 4:30 or 6:30, "depending on whim"; if he carries an attaché case—the slimmer the better; if he plays bridge, "but believes pinochle is the name of a famous children's book."

No Nirvana is more clearly implanted in the public consciousness than the life enjoyed by the Croesus of oil —habitat, Texas. By now most people have heard about the Texan who struck it rich but who had not yet arrived socially. Advised that the sure way to social acceptance was to buy a Renoir and a Jaguar as a start, he ordered one of each. A few days later his wife called him at the office to say that one of the purchases had arrived. "Which one, the Renoir or the Jag?" asked the oilman. "How should *Ah* know?" answered the bewildered wife.

There is truth, of course, in some of the fables from the Southwest. But when it comes to having a really good time, two of the richest oilmen of them all, Clint Murchison and Sid Richardson, will take off for the Koon Kreek Klub. Koon Kreek is a simple fishing encampment outside Athens, Texas (about seventy-five miles from Dallas), where the millionaires swap stories across a kitchen table

12

at dawn, then putt-putt around a well-stocked lake with hooks baited for fish known as bream (pronounced "brim" in Texas). Bream are so small and spiritless that it's hard to tell when one is on the hook. Yet Clint Murchison insists: "I've been trout fishing in France, and salmon fishing in Canada, but there's no fishin' in the world that beats bream fishin' right here in Texas."

Murchison can have his fish, as far as Crawford Greenewalt, president of E. I. du Pont de Nemours, is concerned; Greenewalt prefers birds. Aside from running the biggest chemical company in the world, and qualifying as a part-time classical scholar, Greenewalt is a recognized ornithologist. He is a highly regarded photographer of the life and times of the hummingbird, and as any amateur bird watcher can attest, the hummingbird is about the hardest bird in the world to watch, let alone photograph.

To many, the thought of life at the industrial summit brings visions of capped and uniformed maids, liveried footmen, and kitchens staffed by continental chefs. But have a look, for a minute, into the Cleveland home of Dwight P. Joyce, $125,000-a-year president of the giant Glidden Co. (paints, chemicals, Durkee margarine and other foods).

It is 5:30 A.M., and Joyce is in the kitchen making his own breakfast—a glass of fruit juice, a fried egg, a cup of coffee. "I found years ago that I could get by on six or seven hours of sleep, whereas my wife needs nine," Joyce explains. "So we worked out a system under which I get my own breakfast." For two hours every morning, Joyce is alone, and uninterrupted by the telephone. He spends this time "doing an awful lot of thinking—and not always about business." Sometimes he looks at the sunrise, and pities the people like his wife who are not there to watch it with him; sometimes he thinks about his business colleagues ("The average American businessman is in a rut. He does very little original thinking outside of his own business. He runs with the crowd"). For Joyce, this early-morning session with himself is "a happy time. I don't have to put on an act for anyone. I'm just Dwight Joyce, thinking about myself and my place in the world, and anything that may come to mind."

The early-morning hours are a good deal less leisurely for Edward Cole, the intense and handsome general manager of G.M.'s Chevrolet division. As befits the man who produces more cars than anyone else in the world, Cole's whole life is a closely engineered affair. "I've got my house organized like an assembly line," he says. An electric clock-radio awakes Ed Cole to the news every morning at 6:30, and from that moment on the Cole chassis is on its way down the assembly line. From his bathroom, Cole moves to a "dressing area" where he has arranged the drawers in his bureau so that he hits his underwear first, his socks next, and then his shirts. Moving smoothly down the hall, Cole picks up a tie, puts on his shoes, then drifts by a closet that holds nothing but trousers. Still on the move, he selects a pair and puts it on. Gliding into the main part of the house, the Cole chassis is then fitted with its body shell, at a twenty-foot closet that contains Cole's suit coats (Cole claims he has never yet selected a jacket that did not match the trousers picked up at an earlier stage on the assembly line). From this point it is but an easy step to the next station for fueling up the engine in the breakfast room. Then the product moves on to final inspection and quality control—a quick check by Mrs.

Cole to make sure the coat matches the pants. Cole picks up his overcoat and hat in the hall, and by 7:15 he is driving down the road from Bloomfield Hills to Detroit.

In the realm of ideas, no less than in the area of high living, the top men of U.S. business have been type cast as few other groups in the world—and the image is none too flattering. According to the familiar stereotype, they are rock-ribbed conservatives who can spy a socialist at the drop of a union press release. In some cases, this image is accurate, of course. But listen to salty-tongued Justin Dart, president of the Rexall Drug Company and a hard-working Los Angeles Republican of the "modern" stripe: "If I could abolish all the unions in this country with a sweep of my hand, I wouldn't do it. God Almighty, they keep business in line. But we're concerned with the balance." Dart believes that "we're in a socialist era, and I choose corporate socialism to state socialism. You might say that I'm a corporate socialist. I want every benefit for our employees that our productivity can create." Dart adds that he is "as reactionary as circumstances permit." But judging from what he says, he doesn't think the circumstances permit much reaction these days.

For years, the businessman was the heart of American isolationism, and a few such heartbeats still can be detected in industries now threatened by a flood of cheaper foreign products ranging from chemicals to textiles and cameras. It is not surprising to hear such an internationalist as International Business Machines' president Thomas Watson, Jr., argue for freer trade. "The U.S. is going to be in a hell of a mess," he says, "if we don't accept the thesis that anything that can be manufactured cheaper in Eu-

**15**

rope should be allowed to be sold here for less." Nor is it surprising to hear former chairman Philip Reed of General Electric argue similarly against protectionism. What *is* surprising is to hear a leader of a high-tariff industry— who himself has been burned by foreign competition— speak out *against* high tariffs. Such a man is president Charles H. ("Chuck") Percy of Chicago's Bell & Howell— a camera company. "I think they're very impractical people, these protectionists," says Percy. "We say we believe in free private enterprise, but we don't mean what we say when we plump for high tariffs."

How much of what they say—or what is said for them— do these top men of business really mean? Through their companies, most of them belong to the National Association of Manufacturers. Yet while the N.A.M. once was the voice of big business, it is no more. One after another, the No. 1 men attack both it and the U.S. Chamber of Commerce—for what they are, as much as for what they are not. "Mouthpieces like the N.A.M. and the U.S. Chamber just aggravate the situation," says A.T. & T.'s president Frederick Kappel. "People are tired of the feuding." President Joseph Block of Inland Steel adds: "I don't think the N.A.M. has any following." Motorola's president Robert Galvin says: "The N.A.M. and the Chamber are identified with prejudice and therefore are not believed."

What emerges from all this—from the quiet and thoughtful steelman, the gum-chewing, khaki-clad banker, the scholarly hummingbird expert from du Pont, the articulate scientists-turned-businessmen, the automated automan and all the rest—is not a simple line drawing. No such portrait can be rendered. But these top men—or most of them—do share a common *raison d'être,* a dynamism, an optimism, a self-confidence and a real hunger for work which they could not satisfy even if they wanted to, which they don't. Bergson would have called it *élan vital;* plane maker James McDonnell translates it as "vital bounce."

They are, to begin with, among the hardest-working men in the world. Charles B. Thornton, who heads Litton Industries, which has had a spectacular record in the electronics business, is representative of the breed. Sometimes he gets up at 4 A.M. so he can be in the office by five for a few hours of uninterrupted work. "You live it, eat it, sleep it, breathe it," he says. (Thornton often has a sandwich at his desk for lunch.)

President Robert Paxton of General Electric, who lives in Westchester County and commutes to New York, works this schedule: "I get up on weekdays at 5:15 A.M., catch a train about ten to seven, get to the office around eight o'clock and get home again at seven o'clock that night. I am quite aware of the arithmetic involved and find that I average during the five days of the week about six hours of sleep—probably less than I should get."

Sixty-two-year-old Robert Gross, the able and driving chairman of Lockheed Aircraft, gets even less sleep. He was putting in this kind of week in 1958: a flight from Los Angeles to Atlanta to make a speech, then to New York for half a day, then Nashville and Dayton and Philadelphia and then home to Los Angeles. "Damn right it wears me out," he said. "I'm tired as hell. On the one or two nights a week when I'm not out with some ambassador's sister or with someone else my public relations people tell me I must entertain, I go to bed at eight-thirty or nine o'clock." Does he go to sleep then? "Oh, yes—for two hours." And then? "Then I wake up, thinking about the company. I suppose I average a total of four or five hours sleep a night."

The second thing these No. 1 men—or most of them—have in common is that they are happy in their work. "I would not change it for a million dollars a day," says Chicago's Wayne Johnston, who makes $127,500 as president of the Illinois Central. Like Lockheed's Gross, the men at the top get tired and tense, but seldom do they land on the psychiatrist's couch.° For in their work they find the same kind of creative thrill that an artist or a composer or a poet finds in his. "What most people don't realize," says U.S. Steel's Roger Blough, with controlled excitement in his voice, "is that making steel isn't just making steel—it's making jobs, and making a material out of which an automobile, a flagpole or a train can be created. I find the steel business an engrossing, all-compelling type of life." H. S. M. Burns, the president of Shell Oil, reflects: "I enjoy my job the exact same way that Bernstein enjoys conducting the Philharmonic. I think I know how the oil tune sounds—I don't try to play the flute better than the flutist."

The most important characteristic shared by these men (or most of them) is not *how* they work, but *why*. They do it because they must. Their motivation goes far beyond mere personal ambition (although it may start with that), and far beyond a crude desire for wealth (although it may start with that, too). They are driven by the desire for achievement, and their reward is the satisfaction of getting

---

° In a study of ten thousand executives, Life Extension Examiners found that only 13 per cent of them were subject to serious tensions in their jobs—and the better the job, the fewer the tensions.

things done. But the reward is ephemeral, and the goal always seems yards further down the field.

In different words, they express the self-same thought. Says Don Power, chairman of General Telephone & Electronics: "Success is one of those things we never completely reach. The word itself seems to imply a stopping point, a relaxing of efforts, and this would be the greatest danger to any business."

Eugene Holman, chairman of Standard Oil of New Jersey, puts it this way: "I believe every day's sincere effort is a sort of turning point. I would question whether any sincere growing and developing person feels that at any given point he has 'arrived.' "

To S. S. Auchincloss, president of Tracerlab, Inc., "each level reached is only one more place from which to start."

And General Dynamics' dynamic chairman Frank Pace sums it up for all the rest. "We're trying to create a great corporation, not just a good one. A great one!" How is greatness attained? Pace rises from his desk and smacks the fist of one hand into the palm of the other. "The way to achieve and retain greatness is always to be striving for something more!"

Erik Jonsson, who as chairman of Texas Instruments is head of the world's largest maker of transistors, puts his finger on the kind of drive that sets the No. 1 men apart. "All they need is the glimpse of a reasonable possibility of success," he says, "and if they think they're big enough and tough enough to do it, they'll try."

The challenge that Anastas Mikoyan hurled at them and at their country in the winter of 1959 presents the men at the top with the biggest and toughest job that any group of men has undertaken in modern times. Are they big enough and tough enough and wise enough to meet the challenge successfully?

This book does not pretend to have the answers. But by studying these men individually and as a group—and in the context of the changing system in which they live and work—some of the answers may begin to emerge.

The reader will note that in the present chapter and the ones that follow many of the men and situations discussed are in sharp contrast to the classic images of the industrial leader and the industrial society. In citing these men and situations, the intention is not to create new stereotypes; rather, to shatter the old.

# 2.

# FOUR-WHEEL
# DRIVE

IN THE HIDDEN VALLEY, an hour's drive outside Los Angeles, Litton Industries' president Charles
("Tex") Thornton maintains a hideaway where he disap-
pears whenever he can take a day or two away from his
electronics business. His place is a horse ranch, and there
is nothing fancy about it. Thornton likes it because he can
be alone there, and can find time to think.

One day not long ago, Thornton was drinking coffee
in the ranchhouse, and talking with a friend about what
gives one man the drive of ten, and leaves another at the
starting post. "Look at those thoroughbreds out there,"
Thornton said as he pointed through the picture window
to the corral beyond. "Those animals don't make good riding horses, and they don't make good dray horses or cow
ponies. They're bred to race. It's the same with people. It's
something that's born into you."

Like Thornton's thoroughbreds, the top men of U.S.
industry possess the kind of drive and energy that separate
the winners from the also-rans. Yet strangely enough, in
a society based on the profit motive, these staunchest
defenders of private profits are not themselves primarily

motivated by money. Many of them, it is true, quite naturally entertain a healthy regard for the six-digit pay check. For when a man steps into a top job, his pay is likely to accelerate almost to escape velocity. In 1957, for example, A.T. & T.'s new president Fred Kappel saw his pre-tax take rocket up from $51,000 to $187,000, and Jones & Laughlin Steel Corp.'s new president Avery Adams went from $47,500 a year to $178,500—before-tax raises of more than 350 per cent. And when a man holds down a job for years, he can rise to the outer reaches of the fiscal stratosphere. At Bethlehem Steel, for example, which can boast several of the best-paid men in industry, ex-chairman Eugene Grace collected more than $800,000 for his services in 1956 (the recession cut Grace's pre-tax take to $619,036 in 1957).

Yet the promise of more money is not what keeps most top executives coming to the office every day. For one thing, high taxes make a raise almost meaningless; Grace's $800,000-plus probably left him with take-home pay in 1956 of less than $200,000. After a while, as Avery Bullard remarked in *Executive Suite*, cash rewards represent little more than "the chips in the poker game."

This is certainly the way Crawford Greenewalt feels about his own pay as president of du Pont. It is a well-known fact that on Greenewalt's wedding day in 1926, his father-in-law Irénée du Pont gave him 1,000 shares of Christiana Corp., the holding company that owns gobs of du Pont stock. By 1959, Greenewalt owned 4,096 shares of du Pont common (at $250 a share) and 687 shares of Christiana common (at $17,000), for total holdings worth about $13 million. Thus Greenewalt does not exactly depend on his $300,000-odd yearly salary and bonus from du

Pont to keep body and soul together—in fact, he says he turns 91 per cent of it over to the government.*

Nevertheless, Greenewalt's pay check is not without some meaning to him. "Money," he says, "is about the only form of recognition the business community has devised. If du Pont's board of directors came to me tomorrow and said, 'You don't need the dough; why don't you work for nothing for the next five years?' I would be let down. Money is a symbol in the same way that a Nobel Prize is a symbol to the scientists. You can't eat a Nobel Prize. Of course, you can eat the $50,000 that goes with it, but that's not why people want to win one."

This is not to say that everyone who has reached the top is perfectly satisfied with what he makes. Just like lesser folk, some of the top men complain of how hard it is to salt anything away, and clearly would like to make more. Donald Douglas, Jr., president of the aircraft company that bears his father's name, dreams of "owning a ranch, a yacht, and doing more traveling." He makes $100,000 a year and says he has no trouble at all spending it, what with "high taxes plus the standard of living that must be maintained in this position." Oilman George Getty, a billionaire's son who turned thirty-five in 1959, is another $100,000-a-year man who would like to make more. And Patrick McGinnis, who makes $75,000 a year as boss of the Boston & Maine Railroad, concludes that "everyone wants more money." (McGinnis knows exactly what he would

---

* A few years ago, Greenewalt went to his father-in-law with a good-natured complaint. "Look here, Bus," he said. "Here I am president of the same company twenty-five years after you were president. I earn six times as much as you did but I get to keep only half of what you did." Irénée du Pont cracked back: "Well, look at it this way. You're only half as good."

do if he had it: "I'd buy an art museum.")

But in the higher brackets, relatively few express a desire for added income. General Electric's chairman Ralph Cordiner, who was paid $280,000 (plus stock) in 1958, says: "The fact that others get more pay doesn't bother me. When you reach a certain level, an added amount may just affront people." Freeport Sulphur's chairman Langbourne Williams, who makes $131,000 a year, is not bucking for a raise, either (this gracious Virginia gentleman suspects that in some of the biggest salaries the ego factor must figure pretty large). Is more money an incentive for Royal Little, the $200,000-a-year chairman of Textron whose interests range from textiles to electronics? "Hell, no!" Little explodes.

Anyone who has not himself played in the six-digit salary league may find it hard to imagine how such a pay check can be spent. But, for the men who make this kind of money, it's easy. Here is a breakdown of Royal Little's $200,000, as Little reports it:

| | |
|---|---:|
| Uncle Sam | $116,000 |
| Wife's household allowance | 24,000 |
| Support of mother | 18,000 |
| Home improvements | 10,000 |
| Family charity foundation | 20,000 |
| Left for myself | 12,000 |
| Savings | 0 |
| TOTAL INCOME | $200,000 |

Little does not specify how the $34,000 for "home improvements" and "household allowance" is spent, or what he does with the $12,000 "left for myself." But a few years ago, when Conrad Hilton was asked how he managed to spend his hundreds of thousands, the hotel man answered right down to the last penny. His total income, he said, came to $577,222.53. Of that, $352,104.11 went to pay federal, state and other taxes. He gave $80,944.50 to charity and another $36,526.74 to family and friends. He spent close to $20,000 on travel and business expenses, paid insurance premiums totaling more than $11,000, and spent $12,382.27 on club dues and entertainment. Hilton reported that the maintenance of two homes cost him more than $32,000, and his automobile and boat expenses ran to almost $6,500. "My clothing expense," he said, "was $4,171.63." The grand total came to $555,862.57, which meant that Hilton was able to save about $21,000 that year (1948).

Obviously, with taxes what they are at this kind of income level, a few extra thousand do not make much difference. But if it isn't the money, what *is* the incentive for the men at the top? Missouri-born James Cash Penney, who has made and lost millions, and made them again with his chain of J. C. Penney stores, says he left the money motive behind years ago. "I thought at one time $100,000 would be ample," he recalls. "No one in Hamilton, Missouri, had $100,000. But by the time I had $100,-000, my appetite was whetted. Then I wanted a million." Then, says Penney, another motive took over. "I could see this thing was growing. I wanted it to keep growing so that I could give other young men jobs. I learned to give. I wanted to do some good in the world. I got to thinking that money is a by-product, that if you're a success the money will take care of itself. The ambition I had—I couldn't begin to describe it to you. I've never found a substitute for work. People talk a lot about security these days. What I wanted was opportunity."

That was precisely what James McDonnell wanted, too, when he started his McDonnell Aircraft Corp. in St. Louis with twelve employees just before World War II. McDonnell now gets $106,000 a year for bossing 25,000 employees, but he says he didn't set up his company to get a higher income. "It was the urge to put new wine in new bottles. Some people feel the urge to do creative things, and they do them."

The ambition of these top executives is no simple thing. Does it stem, perhaps, from a craving for prestige, power and recognition? Scholarly Leland Hazard, who for years was general counsel of Pittsburgh Plate Glass before he retired to become a university professor, is one among many amateur psychologists who think so. "The wish to be needed or realized," he says, "drives these men to highly engine themselves for a single purpose. This same wish to be needed motivated the Robber Barons, too. It is the same as the wish for power and prestige—it's just a nicer way to say it."

The trouble is, once a man gets to the top, there are not many people who can tell him how much he is needed—at least not without raising suspicions that the praise is mere bootlicking. This bothers more than one boss. "A pat on the back," says Crawford Greenewalt, "is just as important to the president of the company as it is to the laborer." But Greenewalt, like other bosses, seldom gets such a pat on the back "in a way that is unequivocal." Part of the reason, of course, is that a good executive will not let situations arise that demand a grandstand play; if things are running as they should be, there are few opportunities for dramatic feats. Recently Greenewalt read a book called *The Decipherment of Linear B,* which told how a young

English archaeologist managed to decode some writings in clay, said to have been inscribed in the fourteenth or fifteenth century B.C. "What could I have done in my eleven years of running du Pont that you could be that specific about?" Greenewalt asked.

Of course, there are badges of honor that can be won during the ascent to the managerial heights, and some men quite naturally wear them proudly—a simple bow from a headwaiter, perhaps, or maybe an honorary degree; or a listing in *Who's Who in America.*

The archives of *Who's Who* are loaded with stories of men who tried to buy or pry their way into the pages of the big red reference book. One standard technique is "the avalanche." By this method, the eager applicant simply sends *Who's Who* mountains of biographical and genealogical material about himself (in one instance the load ran to two cubic feet, but to no avail). Another favorite ploy is the "chain nomination," often used by public relations men to tout their clients. This is merely a matter of getting a number of people to make the same nomination at intervals of a few weeks or so. (*Who's Who* editors remain unmoved by this one, too.) Then there is the outright bribe, either camouflaged or otherwise. One Texas oil millionaire, who had been asked to submit some biographical material to be used in a lesser reference volume compiled by the *Who's Who* people, sent in the requested information—along with a check for $500 to cover the cost of twenty copies of *Who's Who in America.* "We hope that's what he wanted," publisher Wheeler Sammons, Jr., said later, "because that's what he got, without his name in it!"

The desire for power and prestige may feed the ambition of some men, but not of all. Is it possible that the speed at which a man is running relates directly to what he is running away from? Many of the top men themselves think the answer is yes. Harry Bullis, the former board chairman of General Mills, who had to interrupt his schooling to go to work, is one of these (he keeps a framed motto in his office: DRIVE STRAIGHT AHEAD WITH A POSITIVE MENTAL ATTITUDE). Socony Mobil's slim and handsome president Albert Nickerson is another who thinks that lowly beginnings can beget vitality and drive. Nickerson says the resultant drive can be materialistic, but usually is something more than that. "It cannot be described in terms of a Cadillac advertisement," he says. "It's more a drive toward the feeling a man *is* somebody."

Certainly, there are plenty of top men in industry who started as nobodies—and who had plenty of reason to run away from their pasts. One automobile executive was the son of a drunken blacksmith who used to stumble home at night and beat up the boy's mother. A railroader, who came from a poverty-stricken family, had a widowed mother who worked as a teacher to make ends meet— until she went stone deaf. An aircraft manufacturer had a steelworker father who was out of a job sometimes for a year at a time.

But the running-away theory does not begin to explain the success of many others who came from wealthy families. What of people like hard-working Jack Heinz of the pickle company, or Tom Watson, Jr., of I.B.M., or J. Peter Grace of the shipping and chemical empire? (Grace works so unremittingly that he has been observed, on occasion, dictating to two secretaries at once in the rear lounge of a commercial airplane.)

When cocktail-party conversation turns to bosses' sons such as these, the amateur psychiatrists have a field day. For every boss's son who succeeds, they say, there are a hundred frittering away their lives at the watering spots of the world, counting off the days and years by the spin of the roulette wheel. And the successful ones? Why, they are simply sublimating their egos, desperately trying to claw their way out from under the shadow of a successful father. Or so the theory goes. But Tom Watson, Jr., gives what sounds like a more reasonable answer: "It's a matter of self-respect with me."

Another favorite theory of success has to do with that pet subject of the psychiatrist's couch, the sibling rivalry. Did John outshine brother Bob in school and thus win a favored place in Father's heart? Bob will show *him*—and Bob goes on to become king of the castle in Detroit. But now look at brother John. He has meanwhile made his own untroubled way to the top in Pittsburgh, where drive and energy are no less vital for success.

In scanning the roster of No. 1 men, it is difficult to detect any meaningful brotherly patterns. A few years ago, the newspapers were surprised and delighted to discover that, while Harlow Curtice was soaring to the top of General Motors, his brother Leroy was contentedly working as a paint inspector on the Chevrolet production line, and was perfectly happy to retire as such. A pair of St. Louis brothers, on the other hand, have each made notable successes in two separate businesses—James McDonnell as an aircraft manufacturer, and William McDonnell as head of the First National Bank of St. Louis and a president of the U.S. Chamber of Commerce. Then there are the two Boston brothers—Robert and Courtlandt Gross—who have

been working happily in tandem for years, first as investment bankers, later as the team that built Lockheed Aircraft.

If brother or sister isn't the source, is it possible that
drive can be taught at mother's (or father's) knee? Many
of industry's leaders talk fondly of their parents, particularly of how their fathers preached the basics of hard work.
"When I was eight," J. C. Penney recalls, "I had holes in my
shoes, so I asked my father to buy me some new ones. But
my father said, 'No, you're old enough. I expect you to
buy your own clothes.' It might have been necessity; we
were poor. But I think he did it to *try* me." By working in
the fields, Penney earned $2.50, and bought his shoes. He
now looks back on that day when he was eight as the moment he got his start in business.

Mulling over all the theories of the amateur psychologists
—the sibling rivalries, the parental influences, the family
background, the childhood environment—the men who
know compulsions best can do little more than conclude
that a person either is born with drive and energy, or he
isn't. As Crawford Greenewalt says, "It's a matter of genes
and chromosomes."

Given the inbred energy and drive of thoroughbreds,
the top managers are not ones to wait for opportunity to
come knocking. They keep the door wide open, and they
are not the slightest bit surprised when opportunity
throws itself around their necks.

Whether they start with one company and stick it out
to the top, or move from job to job, they sponge up experience and store it away for future use. A.T. & T.'s Fred
Kappel, who began as a post-hole digger with a crew of
linemen, was forever being "plucked out of something I

knew about and dunked in another field. This got me exposed to an ever broader group of problems, and an ever broader group of people." One trial by fire that Kappel has always been grateful for was the emergency work he was called on to do during the hurricane of 1938. He was working as an engineer for the telephone company in Omaha at the time, and got a call at eleven o'clock one morning from the East Coast, asking for help. "By 1 P.M.," he recalls, "we had representatives of all the railroads in, and by mid-afternoon we had fourteen or fifteen construction crews and equipment on the way east to help out."

The broadening experience that the No. 1 men soak up can come in a thousand unusual ways. For President Arthur Atkinson of the Wabash Railroad, January 14, 1917, is a date never to be forgotten. That was the day when, at the age of twenty-seven, he was put in charge of running Buffalo Bill's funeral. Atkinson was active in the Elks ("I was the youngest Esquire the Denver Elks ever had"), and the Elks had taken over the show. It was his job, in rented silk hat and Prince Albert, to arrange for the funeral procession and for Buffalo Bill's lying in state at the capitol. "Every Indian tribe in the country, every county, every lodge wanted a place in that procession," Atkinson recalls, and he managed to find a place for all of them. "It started at six-thirty in the morning and went on until nine at night."

The early experience picked up by the Southern Co.'s president Harllee Branch was somewhat more mundane, but it had variety. He moved through two careers before going into the utility business, and thinks that each contributed to the kind of judgment he must exercise now. The son of an irascible and highly capable city editor, Branch himself put in some time as a reporter, and credits that experience with giving him "a certain efficiency in evaluating facts, and an improvement in my ability to communicate." Then he became a lawyer: "The law gave me an ability to decide within arbitrary patterns and an ability to sense when I need a lawyer's advice and when I can afford to disregard his advice."

In the process of accumulating experience, many of the top men decide early exactly what they want, and set their course accordingly. Of all the men who knew what they wanted, few had a clearer idea than Don Mitchell, president of General Telephone & Electronics. He told a friend twenty-five years ago about his plan in life. "The first third of my life," Mitchell said, "I spent getting educated. The next third I will spend becoming financially independent. And the final third I'll spend doing just what I like to do." Mitchell has kept ahead of schedule. He was out of college at twenty-one, president of Sylvania Electric Products at forty-one, in 1946. Sylvania then was doing a $69 million annual business. Mitchell vowed to top $300 million in ten years, and did. Then he decided he wanted a billion-dollar business; and in 1959, by merging Sylvania with General Telephone, he actually did a little better than that. At last report (at a vigorous fifty-four) Mitchell was doing precisely what he likes to do—which is, of course, to work harder than ever.

Some of these men do not go out actively (or at least not consciously) to seek promotion. Nevertheless, to a man, they are always prepared for the next move, and for the one after that. And when the main chance presents itself, they are quick to spot the opening.

President Stanley Allyn of Dayton's National Cash Register remembers exactly such a turning point in his own career. It was The Day the Assistant Comptroller

Wouldn't Let the Soup Get Cold. "A man from the East had been employed as assistant comptroller," Allyn recollects. "As was his custom, Mr. J. H. Patterson, founder of the business, invited a group of executives to dinner at his home to meet the new man." During dinner, Patterson asked the new assistant comptroller to make a few remarks. The new man started, then stopped short. Looking down at the table, he said: "Excuse me, gentlemen, my soup is getting cold."

"By all means have your soup," said Patterson pointedly.

Like everyone else at the table, Allyn knew that the post of assistant comptroller was open again "as of that moment." It was Allyn who got the job, at twenty-six.

As this story so well illustrates, a good deal of luck is involved in the climb to the top. What if the man from the East had decided to let his soup get cold, and made the rafters ring with a paean to National Cash Register, founder Patterson, and the garden spot called Dayton, Ohio? Would he now head the company instead of Allyn?

A man may have the good luck to become assistant to some unusual person who takes a shine to him. There may be a sudden transfer, or an illness—or a death. Not long ago, an executive in his late forties, who was just about to step into the presidency of a major corporation, suffered a mild heart attack. The directors quickly decided that it would be too risky to give the man the job. Instead, they picked another executive in the organization, of about the same age. But for that fluttering heart up ahead, the second choice never would have had a crack at the presidency.

And here is another absolutely vital element in the make-up of the No. 1 man: good health. "With the top three or four jobs," says James B. Black, chairman of

Pacific Gas & Electric, "goes quite a bit of physical punishment. We know that there are many men who are excellent as vice presidents or heads of departments, but who are just unwilling to take the physical punishment of a top job for ten or fifteen years."

Ask any boss what qualities a man should have for a top executive job, and the answer is almost sure to be a list of clichés—character, integrity, competive spirit, leadership, intelligence, ability to get along with people, etc., etc. But surprisingly enough, many a man who seems to have all the qualifications will falter when he faces the big responsibilities. General Electric's president Robert Paxton says: "I have seen innumerable people who by mental capacity, judgment, imagination, ambition and skill have wonderful backgrounds for the taking on of executive responsibilities, but who become distinctly unhappy at being required to make important decisions. . . . These are fine people but they do not make good executives." To Crawford Greenewalt the "feel" of a man is what is important. "The hardest thing in the world to define is executive competence," he says. "But while executive competence cannot be described, it can be recognized. You make a mental integration of a man and you have a feeling about him. The executive's role is like that of a conductor of a symphony—he doesn't play the fiddle or the bassoon, but he can stand up there and get extraordinary results from all these people." It is enough for a music lover to know, says Greenewalt, that Ormandy can conduct beautifully. "When you ask why, you're lost."

Why is it that some people start gasping for breath in the upper reaches of the managerial atmosphere, when they have taken every previous step in stride? Often it is just a matter of intellect, or rather the lack of it. On the way up, a man can compensate for a lack of superior intellect by working harder and longer than his colleagues, or by picking their brains. But there comes a time when he can no longer compensate. That is when his associates begin to realize that he hasn't quite got what it takes, and he begins to know that they know. At that point, like as not, he is finished.

Fortunately for the top men who have to pick top men, a good many people are capable of judging for themselves just what their capabilities and limitations are. By no means does every executive covet the top spot; many are content to settle for second or third best. At General Electric, chairman Ralph Cordiner recently had a top job to fill. He brought in ten men for interviews, explained to each of them the nature of the job, and just how taxing it would be. "I laid it down cold, told them they were doing very well where they were, asked them to think about it, talk to their wives and then let me know. And I told them I'd understand if they turned it down." Of the ten men Cordiner interviewed, six were not sure they wanted to be considered at all.

Some people know from the beginning that they are not cut out for a No. 1 job; others decide along the way. One executive, who made the decision a few years ago and now works as assistant to a No. 1 man, recalls: "Instead of playing first violin, I decided to play the best damn third trombone you ever heard." This man is happy as a third trombonist. But his boss will never settle for anything less than first fiddle—or rather, conductor. For he has the drive and energy and ambition that set him apart.

# 3.

# THE CHANGE:
# CHESS VS.
# CHECKERS

ONE OF THE MOST remarkable facts about today's top managers is that they own so little of what they manage. Time was when the family company, operated as a one-man show, was the rule in U.S. business. That was the day of the spectacular speculator, the derring-do entrepreneur who shot his wad on schemes of his own design and carried them through, for good or ill, of his own accord. What matter if he failed—wasn't it his own money? And what if the public were squeezed or the law stretched? "What do I care about the law?" were the immortal words of Commodore Vanderbilt. "Hain't I got the power?"

But now the king-sized owner-manager has all but disappeared, the curtain is coming down on the one-man show, and the law is looking over the corporate shoulder every minute of every working day. President Fred Kappel of A.T. & T., for one, owned only 236 of A.T. & T.'s 70 million shares in 1959. Chairman Fred Donner of General Motors could claim 23,879 shares of his company's stock—

but that was less than a hundredth of one per cent of the total outstanding. "We chief executives are just employees like the others these days," says President Wilbur Malcolm of American Cyanamid, "although it's taken some of us a while to realize it."

One thing the top men *have* come to realize is that business has become so big and complicated that no single person can run a large company nowadays, any more than the President of the United States can do the job by himself. Dwight Joyce, the early-rising head of Cleveland's Glidden Co., recalls how things were when his father ran the company: "He made all the major decisions around here, and most of the minor ones, too. But when I became president I realized that this was impossible. My father used to ask me, 'What are all these people doing around here? Why, when *I* was running the company I did it with a third the number.' In their era, the rugged individualists like my father did a fine job—but the kind of success they made couldn't be duplicated today. Business has become far too complex. My God! I'd go nuts if I had to make every decision around here. These days you've got to have a lawyer on one side, a tax man on the other, and a financial man over in the corner. You might say that in the old days they used to play checkers; now we have to play chess."

Scattered around the industrial landscape there are, of course, some flamboyant one-man practitioners still to be found. One such is Hollywood's fabled Sam Goldwyn, who boasted in the midst of shooting *Porgy and Bess:* "I'm a one-man institution, a lone wolf. I found years ago that I couldn't do what I wanted to do with a big board of directors. I took in the du Ponts and found I had to explain

**what** I wanted to do instead of just making pictures. I decided I wanted no partner ever again, and I've been independent for more than forty years." (Goldwyn is such a "one-man institution" that he even disapproves of story conferences, believing that "by the time you're finished you have a scrambled egg.")

In the world of high finance, New York's real-estate juggler William Zeckendorf is another who runs a one-man show. Through Webb & Knapp, of which he is the largest stockholder, he controlled, by a 1959 count, close to half a billion dollars' worth of North American real estate from coast to coast. Zeckendorf once said that he was in the business of "turning peanuts into bananas," and often as not he performs this kind of financial alchemy by phone (he has one installed and constantly in use in his Cadillac limousine—New York license plate, WZ). One day not long ago, he put in a call to Carrol M. Shanks, president of the giant Prudential Insurance Co. "Carrol," said Zeckendorf (as he later told the *Wall Street Journal*), "do you think New York needs a new hotel? Good. Then would you lend me $50 million?" Zeckendorf was soon at work, with a helping hand from Prudential, on plans for a $66 million hotel in the heart of Manhattan. Name? The Zeckendorf, of course.

Perhaps the most famous, and least known, of the lone wolves these days is Howard Hughes, the mystery man who controls some $600 million worth of corporations, including Trans World Air Lines, Hughes Tool and Hughes Aircraft. Hughes is so secretive in his dealings that he sometimes negotiates while piloting a prospect around the desert in his convertible in the dead of night; so unpredictable that he once left Thomas O'Neil, vice president of

General Tire & Rubber, at the controls of his private plane, even though Hughes was well aware that O'Neil had not the slightest idea of how to fly. (O'Neil, a towering athletic type with nerves of iron, survived these "longest few minutes in my life"; it was during this trip that he negotiated the purchase of R.K.O. from Hughes.)

But there are few such rugged individualists of the old school today—and as their ranks have thinned, an interesting switch in the public's attitude toward them has taken place. These days the entrepreneur—when he is observed at all—is likely to be regarded more with bemused skepticism than with admiration. Perhaps this new attitude reflects, in part, the new worship of security, which has been decried so often by so many. No doubt it is a reaction, as well, to the autocratic, shady and downright illegal practices pursued by some entrepreneurs in the past.

Old Henry Ford is remembered for the $5 day, and for his genius for mass production. But he also is remembered as an autocrat. One day years ago, Ford went out to inspect the progress being made on his famed Trimotor plane, and was enraged to see a man in knickerbockers standing on the wing. Ford fired him on the spot. "No man wearing knickers works for me," he said. (The nonplused man in plus fours was James McDonnell, who later went on to start his own aircraft company in St. Louis—the company now charged with building the space capsule to carry the first American into orbit.)

"The public be damned!" cried William Vanderbilt in another era, and even such an enlightened latter-day capitalist as Ford could echo the sentiment by decreeing that the public could have any color car it wanted, so long as it was black.

This kind of attitude—along with the public-be-skinned manipulations of the Ivar Kruegers and Charles Ponzis of the twenties—contributed to the changing public view of the entrepreneur, to be sure. But something else has been at work, as well; it is the new face presented by the men who have replaced the entrepreneurs as the stewards of U.S. industry.

The business leader has changed for the very good reason that he had to change. Because most big corporations are publicly owned today, and under close legal scrutiny, it is only good business to be publicly responsible and to act within the law. Because the world has shrunk, and the slightest tremor along the borders of the Iron Curtain can change the conditions under which goods are bought and sold, it is only good business for management to maintain a vital interest in world affairs. Because the power of organized labor has grown so mightily, it is only good business to approach employee relations with an open mind and a willingness to bargain.

"The chief executive," says Donald David, former dean of the Harvard Business School and now with the Ford Foundation, has been forced "to take a much, much broader view. In the twenties and before, the principal job of the chief executive was the economic concern, the operation of the business. Now the top executive spends relatively little time on that. A fair share of his time is spent on relations with the government and the public, in concern with the attitudes of employees, stockholders and customers."

In this connection, more than one corporation president has been taken aback in recent years to find the lowliest of stockholders daring to claim the floor at the annual meeting to challenge management on matters ranging from its labor policy to the amount of money it pays itself. With stockholders thus emboldened, the chief executives have found it prudent to arrive well briefed at their annual meetings, ready to field the toughest questions.

But is all this merely a matter of good business? Isn't there, perhaps, something deeper at work? Donald David thinks there is. "I think the best of these managers today feel a kind of trusteeship," he says. "Today the morality of business is on a pretty high level."

Economics may or may not determine morality, but it has certainly been a potent force behind industry's transmutation from owner-management to hired-hand management. And among the many economic reasons behind the change none has been more important than the economics of taxation. Towering inheritance taxes have made it impossible for most families to pass their industrial empires down intact, while at the same time heavy income taxes have tapped off funds badly needed for expansion.

Furthermore, the very giantism of business these days, which makes expansion mandatory in order to compete, has caused the demand for money to outrun any single-family source of supply. Besides forcing the old family owners to invite the public in as partners, this corporate elephantiasis has caused the other great shift in management—from the one-man show to a three-ring circus of analysis, consultation, and decision.

There was a time when K. T. Keller, the one-time mechanic who for years headed Chrysler Corp., would go down on the production line and take a machine apart to discover for himself, as he once did, exactly why there was so much vibration in a certain compressor ("Just sloppy assembly," Keller concluded). But now, Chrysler's lawyer-president L. L. ("Tex") Colbert finds that he must know his way around in so many fields that he cannot be expert in all of them.

No longer can General David Sarnoff rely on his judgment alone for the multifarious decisions that must be made these days to keep Radio Corporation of America on the beam. R.C.A.'s president John Burns explains the problem this way: "Many corporations are made up of many businesses now. Here, one minute we'll be talking about space vehicles, and the next about the effectiveness of a particular star in a particular television program."

The late Thomas Watson, Sr., used to run I.B.M. almost single-handed, and few could fault his success. But recently, like many of his contemporaries, Tom Watson, Jr., has been developing a "team" of decision makers, extending down into the organization. "It's true that the proprietor used to get very creative ideas," he says, "but not all of them were good. He rarely said to himself, 'I really goofed on that one.' But now there are many checks and balances that prevent me from thinking I'm right all the time. If I felt I could run this company on a one-man basis, I'd do it. But I know it can't be done." A measure of why it can't (and also of how successful the new team system can be): When Thomas Watson, Sr., died in 1956, I.B.M. was grossing $734 million a year; in 1958, it grossed $1.2 billion.

Examples of this sort can be cited by the score. But the profit-and-loss statement can never give the answer to the worrisome question of what has been happening to the human being in this trend to corporate bigness. Is the individual, in truth, being swallowed by the hydra-headed monster? So it is often charged, and many of U.S. industry's No. 1 men themselves have joined the chorus. "The 'team' concept of management has tended to eliminate originality and imagination," says National Gypsum's chairman Melvin Baker. "I have seen examples of 'yesmanship' . . . where people have agreed with the 'brass' when they know darn well that the best thing for the company would be to do something quite different." Chairman James Black of Pacific Gas & Electric warns: "People may come to be secure in their own jobs, and tend not to take the responsibility or the initiative or the risk for fear of losing their jobs."

But would the risk takers of yesterday actually have taken the colossal risks that are required by modern business? Would they—or could they—have gambled the kind of money that is needed now to develop commercial atomic energy, for example, with payoff uncertain and far in the future at best? Utility man Harllee Branch, Jr., of the Southern Co., has his doubts. "Our present move into the atomic power field shows no promise of return except in the creation of know-how. I doubt that any individual businessman would have risked a pay-off twenty-five years from now."

Whatever the answer, the fact is that the top men are deeply concerned about the individual being gobbled up. "Business tends to grind people down," says Tom Watson. "The difficulty of being creative becomes greater, and in his late thirties and early forties the average fellow is likely to say, 'I'll just keep my nose clean and stay in my niche.' He figures he'll just keep going along, making his $10,000 or $15,000 a year. We have more of this than we'd like at I.B.M."

It might be argued that I.B.M. in the past inadvertently contributed to this kind of attitude, by requiring its salesmen to conform even to the extent of dressing alike, in dark suits and stiff collars.* But what to do about it now? "The simplest thing is to let them make mistakes," says Watson. "But it's awfully hard to know that a man is going to fail, and let him go ahead and fail, and cost us money."

More and more of the No. 1 men are seeking ways to give the individual his head, to stimulate his initiative, and to impart to the hired-hand manager the incentives of the old-time entrepreneur. Stock options and profit-sharing plans are the most familiar methods, and among the most effective (although some of them so bind a man with chains of gold that he is, in effect, no longer free). Sometimes the appeal for individuality is more direct. In 1958, for instance, Watson sent out a letter to all managers in I.B.M., urging them to approach their jobs with a "small company attitude." Watson implored: "If every employee, and particularly each manager, thinks in terms of 'this is my company' and approaches every situation and decision as if he were the sole owner of the I.B.M. company, then his actions and decisions will reflect what is best for the Company as a whole." Another time, Watson wrote: "Each of us must aim to make his own decisions, and shun the process of decision by agreement of all possible interested parties."

---

* The idea of Thomas Watson, Sr., who believed that the man should not upstage the machine he was trying to sell, and who found the slightest deviation in dress most disconcerting. Watson, Jr., who now usually wears soft collars "as a sign of emancipation," remembers a conversation his father had with one acquaintance. Watson, Sr., found the man pleasant enough, but was unable to concentrate on a single word he said, so distracted was he by the set of the man's watch chain: it traveled diagonally across his vest, from the lower right pocket to the upper left, instead of horizontally.

To get decisions made on an individual basis, the top men also have been pushing to decentralize their companies' operations and to delegate responsibility and authority down the line. No one has done more in this area than General Electric's chairman Ralph Cordiner. "Each division of G.E. is autonomous," he says, "and each manager is responsible for operating decision-making, which leaves the executive office free to concentrate on long-range planning."

General Telephone & Electronics president Don Mitchell has been among the most fervent proponents of decentralization. Get the local plant manager to make the decisions, says Mitchell, and "everyone in that plant, from the receptionist at the front door to the shipping clerk at the rear, knows that the local manager is running things, and not some main office hundreds of miles away. They see it in everything he does; and they also see that what *they* do has a direct effect on what the *manager* does, and that they, as well as he, are *individuals* who have a job to do."

Spreading authority also helps lighten the load. When lawyer John Barr became president of Montgomery Ward in 1955, he found that the old mail order house was so tightly controlled from the top that he was engulfed by petty decisions. Iron-fisted Sewell Avery, who ran the show for years, had insisted that any expenditure of $2,500 or more, anywhere in the organization, had to be personally approved by him. Barr immediately boosted the figure to $5,000 and gave his one thousand retail outlets in every state of the union far more latitude in leasing property and stocking their shelves with goods of their own selection.

At giant du Pont, decentralization has been carried to

the extent that any one of the company's twelve department managers (in areas ranging from paints or explosives to textile fibers like Nylon and Orlon) may spend up to $150,000 on a single project without an O.K. from any higher authority.

But is decentralizing the only way to bring the individual back alive?

President John Connor of Merck thinks he has hit on an even better scheme—let the individuals set their own goals and, in effect, grade themselves on how well they are measuring up. Under Connor's system, which he calls "Management by Objectives," at the end of every year about 150 of Merck's key people (up to and including the president) write up lists of three different kinds of objectives for themselves—general, specific, and personal. For one man, the general objective may be to get his department working more closely with others that it deals with; his specific objective may be (as it was in one case) "to begin silicon production in January and to reach 60 per cent of production capacity by September"; his personal objective may be anything from improving his vocabulary to working more actively in community affairs.

Once the list is drawn up, the man talks it over at length with his immediate superior, who helps him decide whether his objectives are too ambitious or too short in their reach; then there is a mid-year review of the objectives and revisions are made, if necessary, to adjust for any unforeseen circumstances. At the year end, the man's progress is reviewed in light of the objectives that he has set for himself, and he is compensated accordingly. Connor thinks that this system not only gives a man scope and a cash incentive, but helps provide him with "psychic income" as well.

Try as they may, though, the top men cannot seem to find a satisfactory remedy for a virus that has swept through industry as a concomitant of giantism. It might be called committeecoccus, and it is such a pesky bug that most bosses have given up hope of stamping it out; the best that can be done is to control it.

But how? The answer seems to be twofold: (1) Use committees primarily for advice and consultation, and (2) hold one man responsible for a committee's actions. Once a committee decision deteriorates into a show of hands, says the Southern Co.'s president Branch, "the majority is more likely to be wrong than a thoughtful minority." J. P. Levis, chairman of Owens-Illinois, says that his company "has many committees which are largely for the purposes of discussion and information [but] final decision rests with the individual responsible. . . . It should never be a case of the majority ruling."

Thus, to Stephen Potter's stable of gamesmen, lifemen and one-up-men, must now be added the deftest character of them all, the committeeman. "It takes skill on the part of the committee chairman," explains du Pont's Crawford Greenewalt, who heads the executive committee of that huge corporation. "The skill of the chairman is in making sure that all points of view come out. You've got to encourage the reluctant speaker, but the guy who wants to talk all the time must be graciously shut up."

The committeecoccus virus has flourished because there are few simple decisions to be made in industry these days. Is it a matter of new financing? A platoon of lawyers must make sure that every *i* is dotted and every *t* crossed to conform with the securities laws; a squad of financial men must determine the state of the stock or bond market; a detachment of public relations men must be deployed to

**47**

make sure the new issue gets its due in the public prints, and that the company's stockholders fully understand the need for new money and approve the method of raising it. Is there a merger in the works? Call in the lawyers and find out how the trustbusters in Washington may react; call in the personnel man to see how the newly acquired employees will fit in with the old hands; call the cost accountants and production men to see which operations can be blended into which plants.

The biggest decision that industry has made of late is Detroit's new venture into smaller, cheaper cars—a move that cost the automobile companies some two hundred million dollars. The story of how this decision was made tells a good deal about how industry works these days and provides a strong answer to those who take the black view that the individual is forever hopelessly lost in the corporate maze. Was it the product of committee work, or of individual inspiration? The answer seems to be both.

Into this multimillion-dollar decision went every process of analysis, consultation and review that management these days is heir to—plus a spark of individuality proving that even in the biggest manufacturing corporation of them all it is possible for a man to think and act independently. General Motors' new small car, the Corvair, was the dream of one man above all, and it was largely through this man's efforts that the company was able to start production when the time seemed ripe.

At General Motors, as at all the other automobile companies, platoons of research men and economists are constantly studying how G.M.'s various makes are selling in the market place, and how they may sell in view of whatever general economic conditions may be shaping up. A few years ago, the market analysts began to detect an interesting development: Small foreign cars—including those made abroad by both General Motors and Ford—suddenly were beginning to sell better in the United States. When the men in Detroit first noticed this change, they started to take the market apart—and the foreign cars, as well. They tested the engines, the springs, the transmissions; they knocked them down to see how much it would cost to produce each part in the United States. They put their consumer-research people to work exploring the market— finding out what features Americans liked in the little cars and what they didn't like. Did they complain about the leg room in back? Mark it down. Did they object to the egg-beater noise of the engine? Make a note. Did they think the cars too light? Too small? Too slow? "We came to some conclusions about what the market would be like if we got into it," says General Manager James O. Wright of Ford, "and what it would be like if any of our competitors got into it, or if all of them did. We segmented the market, and found out who was buying these cars, and where they were being bought, and when."

While all this was going on at Ford, Chrysler and G.M. —in fact long before it started—something else was going on in the head of Chevrolet's general manager Ed Cole. His dream began in a Cleveland hotel room in 1950.

At the time, Cole was working as an engineer in the Cadillac tank plant in Cleveland, turning out weapons for the Korean War. There had been an interest in small cars at G.M. for years. "Right after World War II," Cole recalls, "there was a lot of fear of a postwar recession, and many at General Motors felt that there would be a need for a reduced level of transportation. But the recession didn't

develop until 1949—and then came Korea, which short-
ened that one. The result was that the small-car plans of
1946, which were brought along to an advanced stage,
were shelved."

But not by Cole. He still thought that one day a smaller
car would make sense, and in his Cleveland hotel room at
night he secretly started sketching design layouts and components for his dream. "Some of the ideas that were used
in this project resulted from our work with tanks at Cleveland," Cole says. "I had been very skeptical of air cooling,
for instance, but it became evident from our work in tanks
that we could do this thing."

By chance, Cole had hardly completed his drafting-
board sketches for the new car when he was transferred to
Chevrolet in Detroit as chief engineer, and, later, general
manager. He seized the opportunity to set up a research
and development group to work on his new approach to
the light car, among other things. Few at the top corporate
level of G.M. knew exactly what Cole and his colleagues
were up to, but they had given him a budget big enough
to bring the car along through various stages of development. Finally, in the summer of 1957, Cole & Co. had created a full-scale Fiberglas and chrome model. They decided the time had come to show it to their boss, Harlow
Curtice, then president of G.M.

It was no secret that Curtice was less than lukewarm to
the small-car idea; he had often expressed his reservations,
both privately and publicly. What would his reaction be
now?

Curtice was ushered into the super-secret styling room
where Cole's dream had been becoming reality. For what
seemed to Cole like hours, Curtice uttered not a word. He

just walked around the car, inspecting it from every angle, running a finger along a fender, over the roof, along a side panel. "Then," says Cole, "Mr. Curtice launched into one of the damnedest sales talks I've ever heard—on why we should go ahead with the development of the car."

There was a meeting of the General Motors board of directors a few days after that momentous viewing, and Curtice insisted that the board be shown the car. "Their reaction was terrific," Cole reported later. The decision was made to go ahead.

Cole and G.M. forthwith embarked on one of the most elaborate diversionary operations ever launched in industry. The object was to keep the small-car project secret from the public for as long as possible, lest consumers stop buying G.M.'s current offerings in anticipation of things to come. Cole concocted an intricate ruse. He organized the small-car development as if it were simply a plan for a new "Holden 25," an automobile that General Motors produces in Australia. At Cole's behest, G.M.'s Australian subsidiary sent in phony specifications for its mythical new car, and for months kept asking for progress reports on how the various components were coming along. To muddy things still further, Cole and his cohorts then "leaked" these cabled inquiries, along with the answers, to people around the company.

Detroit is a city of rumors, and as usual the rumors flew. But so far as the press was concerned, Cole's cover-up was successful.* One reporter who went to investigate the rumors reported back to his editor: "There's not a word of

---

* Until March, 1958, when Newsweek's Detroit Bureau Chief James C. Jones broke the story that G.M. and Ford were both well along on small-car plans.

truth to them. Why, I was sitting right next to Ed Cole when he got a cable from the Australian manager to check on the progress of the new Holden." The cable, of course, had been carefully arranged by Cole in advance of the reporter's visit.

It may well be, as the *Saturday Evening Post* once said, that Detroit's Big Three first scrutinized the small car "much as the first python must have examined the first porcupine—with surprise, repugnance and a degree of dismay." It may well be that because of the money and the complex decision-making involved they were slow to respond. But in the manner of most publicly held corporations today, in the end they decided that what a large segment of the public seemed to think was best no doubt would be best for them, as well.

Is it possible to retain individuality in the day of hired-hand management and corporate giantism? Perhaps not for all. But the doubtful should not forget the story of Ed Cole and his Corvair. "We have found a way to combine group management with individual initiative," says G.M.'s chairman Fred Donner, "and to apply that to a fast-moving business, and we've had a pretty good result."

And is it possible to retain the kind of bursting enthusiasm that distinguished the owner-managers of yesterday? A few months before Cole's new car was due on the market, a reporter asked to see the Fiberglas model. "I wouldn't do that to you," Cole shot back with a wrap-around grin. "You wouldn't be able to sleep until you owned one."

# UP FROM
# SOMETHING

In this age of giant corporations, what has become of the American dream? Is it still possible for a pauper to become a merchant prince?

As it happens, a better question might be, How often has such a transformation taken place in the past?

From Jack on the beanstalk to John Jacob Astor, the storybooks are full of men who, like Jack, found riches in a castle in the sky or who, like Astor, trapped the Golden Fleece. But the fact seems to be that, in America's industrial society, the rags-to-riches cycle seldom is completed in a single generation. What people tend to remember are the spectacular sagas of success; what they tend to forget is that even the small-town-boy-who-made-good more than likely was the son of a leading citizen of his old home town—the local doctor, or lawyer, or teacher, or preacher.

There have always been exceptions, and no doubt there always will be. The story of David Sarnoff is perhaps the most familiar—the immigrant lad who became a wireless operator and rose to the top of the Radio Corporation of America. Less well known but almost as remarkable is the up-from-nothing success of Henry Crown, son of a Chicago necktie salesman, who put together a gigantic building materials business and ended up owning the Empire State Building. In the same tradition, there is the saga of J. H. ("Dutch") Kindelberger, who like his father started in the steel mills, then rose to the top of North American Aviation. And then there is the tale of Arthur Atkinson, son of a Railway Express messenger, who quit school because of illness and death in his family, and worked successively as paper boy for the Denver *Post*, as usher in the local op'ry house at 35 cents a performance, as elevator boy, as fence rider for cattlemen, and as office boy for a railroad (he is now head of the Wabash).

But most of the No. 1 men do not rise from absolute zero, even if a great many of them can look back on abject poverty. "I have seen the depths of hard times," says the Illinois Central's president Wayne Johnston. His father died when Johnston was an infant; his brother came down with polio; his mother, who had been a schoolteacher, lost her hearing and was reduced to running a boardinghouse to make ends meet. At an early age, Johnston had to go to work. He sold papers, toured the neighborhood grinding ice cream freezers for a fee, worked as a dishwasher and a package wrapper. But Johnston was of well-educated stock—his grandfather had been a teacher, too—and somehow the family got along while he worked his way through college. He studied railroad administration, and soon after graduation went to work for the Illinois Central.

In case after case of poor-boy-strikes-it-rich, there is a similar family background of education and respectability. The family of retailer J. C. Penney was poor, to be sure. But his father—who sent him into the fields to earn a pair

54

of shoes at the age of eight—was a Baptist preacher in Hamilton, Missouri, and thus enjoyed a certain standing in the community.

The story of one of the most successful Texas oilmen also starts with a respectable small-town background, and continues with a similar shove from Papa. Algur Meadows, who as chairman and chief stockholder of General American Oil Co. is now worth some $100 million, was born in Vidalia, Georgia, the son of a doctor. "We had a good name but not much money," Meadows says; but there was enough to get him through little Mercer University.

At first, Meadows wanted to be a doctor himself. But instead he took a tempting offer from a cousin who owned a nearby Ford dealership. For a while after that, Meadows and a friend knocked around the South, making their way as waiters, as dock guards in New Orleans, as traveling salesmen, even as stunt men for Billy Rose, who was making movies in Florida at the time. Finally they drifted to the oil fields of Shreveport, where Meadows landed an office job with an oil company. He got married, rented a little apartment, and settled down to work at $185 a month. But his father was disgusted with him. "You don't even know you're alive," he said. "You're not learning anything."

Meadows took the doctor's advice. He enrolled in a law course, passed his bar exams in two years, then joined another friend in a small loan company which soon burgeoned into a thriving business—until the Depression struck. It was then that Meadows hit on a new scheme of striking it rich in the oil business—not by striking oil himself, but by exploiting what others already had struck. He developed the complicated financial device of selling "oil

**55**

payments"—that is, promises of future production from fields already being developed. Now well on his way to his second $100 million, Al Meadows long ago concluded that "the most important thing in the oil business is finance. It will take all the cash you have and all you can borrow. And you've got to have a long life. Some people hit it early and lucky, but most don't."

While the climb from the very bottom to the very top of the social and economic heap is a rarity, this does not mean that the American dream has never existed, nor that it does not exist today. What it *does* mean is that there normally is a pause of a generation or two—in blue collar, then in white—before the rags-to-riches cycle is complete.

This has always been so. What is heartening today is that the cycle may be shortening. A few years ago, sociologists W. Lloyd Warner and James Abegglen conducted an exhaustive survey among eight thousand top executives to find out where they came from, what their families were like, and whether the land of opportunity was living up to its reputation. Not only did they look into the backgrounds of the men then at the top of American business; they also compared them with the generation that had gone before.

Their conclusion, summarized in the book *Big Business Leaders in America,* was that "men from factory, office, shop and farm backgrounds are now able in greater numbers to achieve top-level positions in American business than a generation ago. . . . All evidence indicates that in American society opportunity continues to be realized, and increasingly so. Rather than closing in on men of low birth, holding them to positions into which they are born, our social system continues to make it possible for men from all levels to move into elite positions in commerce and industry. . . . Admittedly, only a small percentage from the bottom climb to the top, yet this percentage since 1928 has almost doubled."

As Warner and Abegglen pointed out, a major reason for the change has been the inheritance tax (already discussed in another chapter) and its crippling blow to family control of big business. At the same time, the explosive growth of the corporation has been creating thousands of new openings for top managers—far more than the so-called birth elite can ever hope to fill. At du Pont alone, for example, someone once figured out that there is a promotion in the managerial ranks every ten working minutes, or more than twelve thousand supervisory promotions a year.

Since World War II, still another massive force has been opening doors into the corporate hierarchy—the G.I. Bill of Rights. By enabling millions of servicemen to go to college—many of whom ordinarily would never have donned a cap and gown—the G.I. Bill has certainly made way for a great infusion of men from every social and economic level into industry's topmost ranks.

How many from how low a level?

That will not be known for another ten or fifteen years. But that they are coming is certain; battalions of them are on the march.

Despite this certainty, some of the top men still argue about how important a formal education may or may not be in a corporate career. One of them, who took International Correspondence School courses but got no college degree, asks: "What the hell would I have done with a college education?"

But while some bosses may talk this way, it should be noted that their personnel directors do not. "Where did you go to college?" is the first question asked of the job applicant these days, and if the answer is, "I didn't go," the personnel man's eyes are likely to glaze over with a thousand-yard stare.

Compared with the rare individual who clambers to the top from absolute zero, the man who makes the rise from practically nothing is a familiar figure. But this man, no less than the other, must be able to take seven-league strides without ever missing a step. At every step along the way, he acquires new manners of speech, of dress, of thought; at every step, he leaves something behind—his parents, perhaps; his friends and old associates, his old neighborhood, his church, his club, his Thursday-night bowling team.

For most of the men who hit the top, such parting is neither sorrowful nor sweet, but simply a fact of life. Many of them are so engrossed in their work that they have little desire to develop outside attachments. Others are moved about so often that they cannot. For good reason, psychologists refer to them as "men who have left home" both physically and mentally.

General Electric's president Robert Paxton "left home" physically at the age of two when he was brought to the United States from Scotland. He talks of his success this way: "Many very able men, possibly far more able, have had distractions which I did not have at some rather critical periods. I have not had the good fortune to have children, and consequently this particular distraction away from business did not occur. Being an immigrant with very few relatives in this country, and having been moved rather frequently from location to location as a youngster,

I suppose that I built up fewer than the usual number of close friends so that there was little social interference with my time. Similarly, there were no periods of long family illness which would have obligated me to adopt a more conventional allocation of my time. I hope, had any of these or other situations existed, I would have behaved as a normal human being. My point is that they didn't occur, so it became relatively easy for me to almost live my work."

The endless series of arrivals and departures that are part of the great American success story, in the opinion of Louis Kronenberger, have contributed to a peculiarly American brand of conformity. "The very gospel of Getting Ahead," he wrote in his book *Company Manners*, "imposes a special need for conforming: one almost has to conform because the pace one moves at, and the always new country one is moving through, leave one too insecure and ill-informed to strike out for oneself."

One might argue, with some reason, that the conformity is a surface veneer. But Kronenberger's description of the road to riches rings true: "Americans, in the course of moving upward, must again and again wear different clothes, eat different food, belong to different fraternal orders and then country clubs and then city clubs, take on subtly different opinions about marriage and divorce, politics and art, sport and education; they must keep up with fewer and fewer people, but keep up more and more appearances."

Kronenberger does not contend that this is *all* bad, for it is true that in the course of corporate advancement a man has a look at and a taste of a broad slice of life. He may see America first—or South America. "The white hopes are shifted from department to department, even from continent to continent: from being in charge of sales in Rio they pass to being in charge of personnel in Rome; now they are assistants to the president of their corporation, now they are on loan to the President of their country; it is their job today to sit around and listen, tomorrow to go out and speak."

While the growth of business and of the inheritance tax has created more and more opportunities for men to rise to the top, one event of the past generation made it possible, or rather necessary, for more men to rise from close to the bottom. This was the Great Depression, with the leveling force of an economic H-bomb. No one has to be reminded of how, in the thirties, families in comfortable circumstances—families in a fair way, in other words, to produce the business brass of the next generation—saw their standards of living crumble, their possessions vanish, their hopes evanesce.

What happened to the potential No. 1 men who were children during the Depression years? For the most part, they are just now beginning to appear in the upper levels of management. Some have already hit the top, and among these, few can claim a more amazing biography than Charles Percy, who earned his first pennies hawking magazines on the streets of Chicago at the age of seven and became president of the Bell & Howell camera company when he was only twenty-nine (he just turned forty in the fall of 1959).

A five-foot-eight-inch package of energy and enthusiasm, Percy can remember the day when his father, a cashier in a small neighborhood bank, lost his job in the crash. And he can remember the days and months and years after that, when the Percy family had to move thirteen times, each time to a cheaper place because they couldn't pay the rent. On occasion, Percy was sent down the street on a cold winter night to borrow oil from a neighbor, because the Percys couldn't buy their own. He remembers taking typing lessons in junior high school, and spending the evenings typing out a hundred letters to banks asking for a job for his father (there were no takers).

Even before the crash, Percy was hustling; from the day he was seven, he says, "I never took a cent from my parents." He started by selling magazines. He took three copies of the *Saturday Evening Post* the first week, and sold them. He took four the next week, and sold them—then five and six and so on until he was selling 150 magazines a week by the time he was eight. He branched out to the *Ladies' Home Journal* and *Country Gentleman,* and one week won an award for selling more copies of *Country Gentleman* than had ever been sold before in an urban area (the figure was six). "I used to get home late," Percy recalls. "I was always trying to beat myself."

At eleven, he started selling papers, and his income soared to $5.50 a week. Then he started a shopping service for housewives on Saturdays, and for a while he managed to hold down three jobs at once, while keeping his school grades up.

It is not unusual for a boy to work his way through college. But Percy did something more: *Before that, he worked his way through elementary school, junior high, and high school, too.*

He enrolled at the University of Chicago, where he waited on tables for eight or nine hours a day—until he was struck with an idea that was to change his life. "I realized that I just couldn't do it all with my own two hands," he says. "I realized that I would have to organize the work of others." So Percy set up a purchasing agency to supply the university residences and fraternity houses with food, coal, furniture and linen. By his senior year, he was clearing $10,000.

While Percy was scrambling, so was his father. He got a series of jobs, ranging from automobile salesman to statistician, but the income was small and irregular at best. Finally, he became a night clerk in a hotel. He worked twelve hours a night, seven nights a week, for $35; the rest of the family, as a result, never saw him.

Then, one day, the older Percy got a decent, daytime job—as an accountant for Bell & Howell. It meant that for the first time in months he could see his family; it meant that for the first time in years he could see a future for himself. "Naturally," says Percy, "Bell & Howell became a symbol to us of something that was pretty good and fine."

At the end of his freshman year, young Percy marched into Bell & Howell himself and landed a job as a summer trainee, and at the end of the summer he wrote a report recommending that his job be abolished. This so tickled Bell & Howell's president Joseph H. McNabb that he asked Percy to come back the next year. But instead, Percy went to work for the Crowell-Collier Publishing Company. He was a retail representative, which meant that his job was to tour the newsstands, shuffling Collier's and other magazines to the top of the pile for the best display. The pay was $50 a week.

Percy called on seventy-five newsstands his first day, a record that impressed his boss but did not endear him to his four fellow "retail reps" in the office, who liked to take in a ball game any afternoon they could. "In this job," they told him pointedly, "it's impossible to make more than thirty calls a day." Percy explained that as long as he was getting $50 a week, he planned to do the best job he could.

Soon Percy's boss was holding him up as an example to the others, suggesting that if they couldn't meet the Percy record they should pull out. This did not help Percy win any popularity contests, either. But at the end of the summer, he says, "an amazing thing happened. Those other men took me out to lunch. They were all working harder than ever before by then, and they were all in line for better jobs as a result. They said they were getting more out of life, and they were happier. They took me to lunch to thank me. I was so enriched by that experience that never since have I hesitated to ask an honest day's work from anyone."

When Bell & Howell's president McNabb learned, at the end of that summer, that Percy had gone to work for someone else, he called him to his house and asked him why. Percy explained it was the difference between $16 a week and $50. "Chuck," said McNabb, "I never want money to stand between you and Bell & Howell again. Next summer, you come back to us, and we'll pay you $55 a week!" Percy took the offer, and when he got out of college in 1940 he went to work for Bell & Howell full-time. He was put in charge of defense contracts, which soon became the major part of the business, and after a tour of duty with the Navy he was made a director of the company. When McNabb died in 1949, twenty-nine-year-old Percy impressed the Bell & Howell directors as the natural choice for the presidency (Percy's father worked for him as office manager for eight years until he retired at the age of seventy-five).

Thus, to the usual burdens of assuming the presidency of a company, another was added in Percy's case: He was a boy wonder, too. This is not an easy role to play, and most boy wonders, after a few years in the limelight, would be happy to have people forget their age. One of the best-known whiz kids of recent years was Charles Luckman, who became president of Pepsodent at thirty-four, and Lever Brothers at thirty-seven. He had a falling-out with the Lever directors in 1949, and since then has established himself in another highly successful career, as an architect on the West Coast. But his memory of his boy-wonder days remains as fresh as a cake of soap.

"An aurora borealis builds up around your name," he says. "I suppose my obituary will read, 'One-time boy wonder.' In the days when I traveled with Bob Hope, when he was doing shows for servicemen, people used to come up to him and say, 'Be funny, Bob.' " In the same way, Luckman says, the boy wonder forever is being approached by people with an expectant look that seems to say, "They tell me you're amazing. Amaze me."

It is not surprising, in view of this, that Percy, like most other boy wonders, is sick and tired of being regarded as one. But in his campaign to have people forget his age, he is handicapped by the fact that he looks about ten years younger than he is.

Whether or not his own five children will ever have to face this particular problem, Percy does not plan to let them grow up without learning the lessons he taught himself. Every week he designates one of his children "captain" of the house, and one of the captain's chores is to make sure that the whole family is awake by 6:45 A.M.

It happens to be especially important for no one to over-sleep in the Percy household, so tight is the schedule. At 7:15 there is a family meeting, when songs are sung and the Bible is read; then there is breakfast; and then, from 8:05 to 8:20 every morning, Percy takes a French lesson (because he thinks that Americans doing business abroad ought to be able to speak at least one foreign language).

What happens when the "captain" of the house over-sleeps? "Why, then his allowance is docked," says Percy. "I've got them all on incentives at home!"

Percy's own incentives have changed since he has risen to the top. "I don't need any more money," he says. "I get a thrill out of contributing—to the university, to boys' clubs and so forth. I often think about Mr. McNabb. This man believed in people. He was interested in my father, a man in his fifties, and he was interested in an eighteen-year-old kid like myself." Percy hopes that he has developed the same kind of interest in people.

Often, too, he thinks about the days when his father was struggling to keep the family together, and Chuck was scrounging for nickels and dimes on the streets of Chicago. He does not regret a single minute of that experience. "The greatest thing that ever happened to me," says Percy, "was the Depression."

# 5.

# THE KID IN
# THE BLACK
# VELVET SUIT

FROM THE MOMENT he set foot in the offices of Amalgamated Emulsion & Dye, J. Hornsby Jones III was a marked man. No one (so the personnel director later reported) had ever conducted himself more adroitly in an interview, and no one ever was more clearly qualified for the management training course. J. Hornsby was hired on the spot.

For two weeks "Jay" worked in Amalgamated's mail room, and to hear the office manager tell it the young man had the talents of a postmaster general. Then he moved into Accounting, where (as the chief accountant later reported) he figured out a new inventory system that was sure to save the company thousands. So it went in every department—sales, production, advertising. ("Keen insight . . . quick mind . . . great imagination," ran the ad manager's report on him.) Such a man, quite obviously, was cut out for bigger things, and when his eight-week training program was finished, Jay was haled to the president's office.

"My boy," said the chief executive, glancing over the dossier of glowing reports on his desk, "never in my career at Amalgamated have I seen such a record. Ordinarily, I would put a young man like you in the field for a while, then bring him back to the home office for more seasoning. But in your case I believe this would be a waste of valuable time. I want you to start tomorrow as executive vice president and my personal chief of staff. Congratulations, young fella."

Jay, whose eyes had been cast modestly to the floor, looked up at the president's outstretched hand, and grasped it. "Thanks, Dad," he said.

Next to the farmer's daughter, almost no character on the American scene has been subjected to more sly humor than the boss's son. The funny papers paint him as the kid in the black velvet suit who rides to school in a chauffeur-driven limousine. In the movies, he is the unpleasant brat who snitches on his father's quaking hirelings. He is the lad in light fiction who gets through college on the strength of a new endowment from the Old Man; in real life, he is the luckless chap whom the tabloids delight to FIND IN LOVE NEST. He is the poor little rich boy who turns bad—or the upstart, like J. Hornsby, who vaults over all the rest to a place on the board and in the sun.

The boss's son endures as a butt of American humor because the boss's son is still very much around. Despite the trend away from family-owned big business, strong family ties still entwine even some of the largest, publicly held corporations.

In some big companies, of course, the founding family is still in firm control. The Fords, for instance, still own 11.5

per cent of Ford Motor's stock, and control 40 per cent of the votes; the Heinzes still control H. J. Heinz & Co., the Pittsburgh food producer. And in many other companies, though the founders' ownership has been whittled down almost to zero, the families nevertheless still run the show. Pillsbury Mills, for instance, is headed by Philip Pillsbury, though the Pillsbury family together owns less than 5 per cent of the company's stock. International Shoe, biggest maker of shoes in the country, is bossed by Henry H. Rand of St. Louis, a direct descendant of one of the founders, though the Rand family now can claim less than 3 per cent of International's stock as their own. And at Inland Steel in Chicago, which was founded sixty-six years ago by a group including Joseph Block, grandson Joseph Block is the president today, though he and the other family members now active in the company own only 1.5 per cent.

In view of the national tradition of free and equal opportunity for all, it is no surprise that Americans look upon inherited position with something less than total approval. But is the boss's son really the dolt and slugabed that he is cracked up to be?

Certainly there are those who merit the unfortunate reputation. But many sons of success, contrary to the popular impression, possess the same kind of drive that propelled their fathers to the top—and sometimes in even greater measure. Because of their gold-plated upbringing and their almost assured position in the industrial hierarchy, these men feel a pressing need to prove themselves —to the world at large, to their associates, to their fathers and to themselves. Often as not, they set out to do it by buckling down to a work schedule rigorous enough to test the staying power even of their fathers.

One such man is W. R. Grace & Co.'s forty-six-year-old president J. Peter Grace, who has devoted all his efforts in recent years to diversifying his family company's operations from shipping into chemicals and many other fields. Few men in American business work as hard as Peter Grace (and few, for that matter, work their employees as hard as he does). He puts in an eleven- or twelve-hour day, including two hours of dictation in the car, riding between his New York office and his Long Island home. He takes five or six hours' work home with him every night, but never finishes it. "The deficiency," he says, "is made up on trips when I work longer hours."

Though he makes $250,000 a year for his labors, Peter Grace says money is not an incentive for him. He gets "great satisfaction from the work itself"—and yet, there is something missing. If he had his life to live over again, Grace thinks he would *not* go into his family's business. One reason, he says, is that "when you are the third-generation member of the family, the rest of the family never appreciates anything that you might be able to do for them. Business is tough—it's no kissing game. However, most people who inherit money don't realize how tough it is, since everything they have comes to them pretty much on a silver platter, with the result that they are harsh judges."

But there is another and perhaps more important reason why Peter Grace thinks he would not again start off in the family firm. It has to do with a question that gnaws within many a filial breast. Grace puts it this way: "I never will really know where I could have gotten on my own. Everyone likes to know what he could do against competition with no unfair advantage, such as being assisted by nep-

otism. . . . Everyone knows that in family companies arti-
ficial situations are created."

Like Peter Grace, most bosses' sons are quite aware of
the delicate situation they find themselves in. "The boss's
son is on the spot," says retailer Stanley Marcus, head of
Dallas's Neiman-Marcus store. "He's got to be more judi-
cious and more circumspect, and he's got to have more understanding. He has to earn the respect of the people he's
working with. I think the successful bosses' sons are those
who work doubly hard." Marcus correctly puts himself in
this group. "I realized that I wasn't a genius and that I
would have to work hard to compensate for that," he says.

Another top-drawer retailer, president Richard H. Rich
of Rich's department store in Atlanta, came to the same
conclusion long ago. Rich's was founded by his grandfather shortly after the Civil War, and Rich was steeped in
its tradition from childhood. Everyone in Atlanta knows
that if you buy something you don't like at Rich's you can
always take it back. At Rich's recently, one woman credited
a pair of high-button shoes that had been sitting in her
attic for decades. More than one not-quite-honest Atlantan
has credited merchandise that wasn't even bought in the
store, with no questions asked.

"We've always made a fetish of emphasizing people
rather than things," Rich says. "We don't teach our people
sharp salesmanship, but how to please the customer. If you
please him, then he'll come back."

Rich learned all this and more at his grandfather's knee,
and it was only natural for him to go to work in the family
store. But, as it turned out, he hadn't learned enough. "I was
pulled out of the basement and made merchandise manager of upstairs apparel before I was thirty," he says. "I

made too many mistakes. I bought goods that the public didn't want." The result was that, despite his family connections, Rich was demoted; it was years before he rose to such a height again. "The job of being the boss's son, or a member of the family," he says now, "is difficult to such a degree that I have told my own son not to come into the business unless he's prepared to do the hardest damn job in the world."

In Rich's opinion, the boy must also be prepared to face "a subtle undercurrent of resentment." This always exists, Rich thinks, when any young man is getting ahead—and the resentment is intensified if it's a family member. This kind of chilly undercurrent has been felt by many a boss's son.

Dealing with his fellow employees may be a ticklish problem for the boss's son; but dealing with his father is no less so. Many sons, in fact, have found that the hardest part of the job is getting through to the boss. "Most employees are sycophants to some degree," one boss's son complains. "They will tell father that such-and-such a division of the company is going great even though it may be coming apart at the seams. Being human, Dad likes to hear good news. But I've always considered it part of my job to tell him the worst, even though it's tough to make him believe it, and there's hell to pay when he finally does."

Adding to the delicate relationship between father and son is the touchy matter of pay and promotion, toward which most bosses' sons entertain ambivalent feelings. On the one hand, they don't know where they would be without the beneficent presence of the old man; on the other, they suspect they might be better off than they are. Because of his family connection, says Inland Steel's Joseph Block, "I always had some feeling of rising faster than I might have" (he became sales manager at the age of thirty-four). But then, too, Block had the feeling at times that "people were leaning over backward in the other direction because of my family connection."

Donald Douglas, Jr., of Douglas Aircraft, whose father is chairman of the company, had precisely the same kind of feeling. "A lot of people," he says, "carry the thought in their minds that this guy got a promotion because he's the boss's son. But I've felt actually that I've been held back. . . . Sometimes my father had to play it slow and cool with me. Some of the middle time here, I thought my salary was a little short of what others might have gotten in the same job." At $100,000 a year, though he would like to make more, president Douglas isn't especially unhappy about things now, "but I can't say I've *never* been unhappy."

If the boss's son has his doubts about where he might have landed on the outside, the father-boss often is bothered by similar soul-searchings of his own. Like any other man, the boss likes to see his son succeed—but how can he be sure the success is well deserved?

Sometimes there comes a moment when a son, by some brilliant stroke, can cause all parental doubts to disappear. There is the story, for instance (told by Matthew Josephson in *The Robber Barons*), of how William Vanderbilt won the confidence of his father, the Commodore. One day the younger man needed some fertilizer for his Staten Island farm, and asked his father how much he would charge for manure from his Manhattan stables. "What'll you give?" asked the Commodore cagily. "It's worth $4 a load," said Billy. His father, thinking that this was twice what it was worth, readily agreed, and the deal was set.

Next day, the Commodore saw his son with a scow all loaded and ready to set off for Staten Island. "How many loads have you got on the scow, Billy?" he asked. "There must be at least thirty." The son pretended surprise. "How many?" he said. "Why, one, of course. I never put but one load on a scow—one scowload. Cast off the lines, Pat!" The Commodore was so delighted with this display of acumen that he gave Billy Vanderbilt a small, bankrupt railroad on Staten Island to manage, and ultimately brought him into the family business, the New York Central.

But such genius is not always so dramatically discernible. More often than not, the boss has to rely on what other people down the line tell him about how his son is doing. How can he be sure they are telling him the truth?

Few companies agree on the pros and cons of family relationships. Some take the stand that the more members of the family who come aboard, the merrier. Donald Douglas, Jr., says, for instance: "We have brothers and cousins and sisters and wives all over the company." (The fact that Douglas finds it hard to remember what jobs all his relatives are holding down at any given moment, however, would indicate that they did not get where they are merely on the sufferance of the president or of the chairman.)

At the Pillsbury Company in Minneapolis, a finer genealogical line is drawn. There is now a firm if unwritten company law that no family member can work for Pillsbury unless he bears the Pillsbury name. A few years ago, when a non-Pillsbury cousin tried to get a job with the company, he was advised to look elsewhere (he went to work instead for competitor General Mills, where he has done very well indeed). The Pillsbury theory is that it is good for company morale to have Pillsburys coming to work: It shows that the family still has interest and faith in the old family firm. But to extend this hiring policy to non-Pillsbury relatives, the family thinks, would be to indulge in the rankest sort of nepotism.

Across the Mississippi from Pillsbury—and more firmly on guard against possible nepotism—sits Northwest Airlines, in St. Paul. Northwest's president Donald Nyrop expresses the view of more than a few companies that have no long-standing family tradition. "We will not hire any brother, sister, son, daughter-in-law, or any other relative of anyone in the company," he says flatly, "from the supervisor level right up to the president." Like Northwest Airlines, giant General Motors can hardly be considered a family business, yet no such hard and fast anti-family rule has ever existed there. G.M., in fact, numbers among its top executives Pontiac's boss S. E. ("Bunky") Knudsen, son of G.M.'s late president William S. Knudsen. But General Motors chairman Fred Donner has his own private policy on the matter. He will never let his own son go to work at G.M., he says, because he thinks it would be unfair to the boy.

Whatever the difficulties in the boss-son relationship, few would deny the good that can come of a boss's son joining the family business. To begin with, he brings more knowledge to the job than the ordinary hireling. A case in point is Henry J. Kaiser's son Edgar, who now sits atop the many Kaiser enterprises ranging from aluminum, steel and cement to a worldwide construction business. Henry J. put Edgar to work as a waterboy on construction projects when he was twelve, and began taking him to business meetings when he was fourteen. "I have grown up with the business," Edgar says, and as a result, during his rise to the top, there has been no resentment on the part of other employees (at least none that he has been aware of). "The people with whom I've been working," he explains, "remember me in the gravel pits and in the shops."

When Edgar was in the middle of his junior year at college, he got a call from his father one day: Henry J. had a pipeline to build, and he wanted Edgar to boss the job. The young man quit college to have a try, and never went back to school again. He sometimes regrets not having a degree, but he has never regretted going to work as early as he did. Edgar Kaiser put his own eldest son to work in a gypsum plant the summer he was fifteen, and is only sorry the child labor laws governing interstate commerce prevent him from starting his children to work even younger.

Edgar Kaiser says of his oldest boy: "He can't just come out of school and step into a job. He's got to work his way. If I don't give him the opportunities that were given me— if I tell him to take a trip around the world instead of going right to work when he gets out of college—I would be doing him an injustice. I will know, I hope, whether this boy has the ability to lead. I can't force him. The greatest damage I could do would be to try to force him."

Most father-bosses try to take a neutral stand on what their sons should do when they grow up. Jack Heinz, who is the third-generation Heinz to run the family company (he took over at thirty-two, when his father died), now has a son at Yale. The young man has worked during summer vacation at a Heinz plant in Michigan. But Jack Heinz says he is not bringing any pressure to bear on the fourth generation.

Not all fathers find it possible to remain so neutral, how-ever. Inland Steel's Joseph Block says he had a deep de-sire to go into the newspaper business, but his father persuaded him to join the steel company. And Owens-Illinois's chairman J. P. Levis wanted to be a doctor. "But ours was a family business at the time," he says, "and my family urged me to take an engineering course, which I did. Twice during the early part of my career I contem-plated returning to college and taking medicine. Both times the offer of promotion stopped me from doing it. . . . If I had my life to live over again, I still think I would have liked to have been a doctor."

It is not just for reasons of family pride or a desire for self-perpetuation that bosses urge their sons to come to work for them; they know that there are occasions, partic-ularly in a firm with long family traditions, when only a family member can save the day.

One such opportunity came for Tom Watson, Jr., in his first days as president of I.B.M. His father was then seventy-seven, and young Watson was the only man in top management with a strong technical background. At the time, I.B.M.'s computer division was lagging badly behind Remington Rand, whose Univac was running away with the market. Tom Watson had both the technical knowl-edge and the "feel" of I.B.M. to do the right thing. Since I.B.M. had a tradition of being a one-man company, he decided to pick the strongest man he could find and make him "computer czar." Watson told the man: "You're Mr. Computer for I.B.M." It worked. Before long, I.B.M. was hot on the tail of Remington Rand, and it has since cap-tured the lion's share of the computer market. Having thus successfully used the one-man technique, Watson since has turned the company more and more into a team operation

—the kind of revolution, again, that probably only a Watson could accomplish.

In another company, a big Midwestern firm, the directors recently had to pick a new president, and the logical choice was between two crack men who both had proved themselves over the years. The trouble was that, if either one was chosen for the top job, the other was sure to quit. The directors finally decided to pick neither; instead they reached down the line and gave the job to the founder's son. The happy result was that both the seasoned men stayed on—and, with their help, the founder's son proved capable of handling the presidency himself.

There is probably no more dramatic example of the good a boss's son can do than the story of how Henry Ford II saved his family's company. As World War II drew to a close, old Henry Ford was aging and out of touch; his son Edsel was fatally ill. Thus weakened at the top, Ford Motor Co. faced the complex and massive job of reconverting from war to peace. Charles Sorenson, the production genius who was with old Henry almost from the beginning, became convinced that the company could make the transition successfully only with a Ford at the helm. "To me," Sorenson later wrote, young Henry "meant the future of the company." And so he did. By hiring and firing the right people and reorganizing the company, young Ford stopped the drain on its resources and nursed it back to robust health.

Two of Chicago industry's brightest young men are Charles Percy, a classic example of the man who came up the hard way, and Motorola's president Robert Galvin, a classic example of the man who didn't. Percy and Galvin are close friends. They work hard together in community activities and Republican politics. Each holds the other in high regard. To Galvin, Percy's up-from-nothing rise to the presidency of his company at the age of twenty-nine is nothing less than unbelievable. To Percy, Galvin's success is no less notable. Galvin's father, who founded Motorola, propelled his son to the executive vice presidency at the age of twenty-seven, and the presidency at thirty-four. "Bob had a terrible handicap to overcome," says his friend Percy. "He had a successful father."

A quick tour of the Motorola plant with Bob Galvin indicates that in this company no one begrudges the boss's son a thing. Workers along the production line turn from their jobs to greet him ("Hi, Bob!"). His secretary first-names him, too, and in the plant cafeteria, where he has lunch every day, Galvin banters easily with anyone who happens to be standing next to him on the chow line.

Tall, trim and prematurely gray, Galvin has given a lot of thought to the job of being the boss's son. One day not long ago, sitting in his modern office, he tilted his chair back, propped his feet on the desk, and told a visitor about his conclusions.

"I was keenly conscious in my early teens," he said, "that if I moved into Motorola there would have to be a demonstration of interest in doing a good job. I decided I would be myself, and I've never pushed myself in relation to my associates. I developed a philosophy of working with people, not just having them work for me; I was quite willing to take what came along. Aside from that general philosophy, the next fundamental that I recognized was the fact that I'd have to run a little faster and work a little harder than my senior associates in order to catch up with them."

Galvin started as an apprentice in the Motorola plant,

carrying radio parts from where they shouldn't be to where they should be. He spent twelve years working in every Motorola department. Because he did a great deal of homework—reading up on electronics and studying Motorola's workings—he soon found, he says, that he "was able to stand toe to toe with my associates. To switch the metaphor, I always had the feeling that I was coming to meet the ball a little harder than the next fellow." Nevertheless, he adds, "I don't think for one minute that it wasn't a lot easier for me to get where I am than it would have been if my old man weren't where he was."

It is not often that a father and son in business together think as much alike as do the Galvins. They live close together now, often consult with one another at night, and ride together to work. "People can come in to either one of us," says the son, "and get damn near the same answer."

Bob Galvin does not have to work these days to support his wife and four children. Yet he is so absorbed in his job that some evenings—after he has finished his reading and other homework—he will sit at home with a note pad on his lap, "just dreaming" about better ways to run Motorola, and ways to make the company a better place to work.

Why does he bother?

"I only come to work here because I think it's good for the other people," says this boss's son. "Don't get me wrong. They could take any one of fifteen others who could do my job as well or better. But if I didn't work here I would work somewhere else to make an economic contribution. My guess is that ego is part of the reason: I don't want to do a bad job. But I don't think that's my biggest reason. I humbly think that I can do some good for people by working in this joint."

79

# 6.

# THE PRIDE
# OF THE PRO

*Everybody has to have a philosophy—and my philosophy is that you've got to be a pro. I have admiration for professionals of all sorts—baseball players, toolmakers, even professional cab drivers. I'm a professional manager, and I get my satisfaction knowing it.*

—DAVID LILLY, president, Toro Manufacturing Corp.

FOR MORE THAN HALF a century the big building has stood there, a part of yet strangely apart from the hurly-burly of Times Square. Its red brick and white limestone walls, its graceful Mansard roof evoke another era—a time of horse-drawn carriages and gentle gaslight; a time when men of affairs could, and did, change the course of industry with the wave of a cigar.

The place is the Astor Hotel, and the old building recently has undergone some changes that symbolize the metamorphosis of industry itself. In the famous Astor roof, where, in the thirties, they used to swing and sway to Sammy Kaye and swoon over Frank Sinatra, the bandstand now is quiet. Every eye in the room these days is firmly fixed on charts and tables showing how, by professional techniques, one company is run well, and how others can be.

The reason for the change is that the Astor has become headquarters for the largest management training school in the world, which now occupies almost three floors of the old hotel, including the roof. Its name is the American Management Association, a nonprofit organization whose mission is to spread the gospel of professionalism. A.M.A. preaches that the business of running a business nowadays is as much a profession as medicine, theology or the law.

From the standpoint of the training required for the job, few would dispute the A.M.A.'s position; business has become so complicated that the modern manager needs a solid grounding in subjects ranging from public relations to psychology. And like the doctor or lawyer or preacher, the businessman must keep on learning long after his formal education is completed. But out of the now accepted doctrine of professionalism has sprung a far more controversial corollary—that the professional manager can ply his trade with equal success in any field of endeavor, almost without regard to specialized experience. "He who can manage," says Lawrence Appley, the president of A.M.A., "can manage anything."

It was in this belief, of course (not to mention the corporate prestige that was sure to accrue), that such men as General Lucius Clay (now chairman of Continental Can) and General Douglas MacArthur (now chairman of

Sperry Rand) were welcomed into industry after their long and distinguished military careers. When the late General Brehon Somervell was named president of Pittsburgh's Koppers Co. in 1946, a friend asked him: "How can you do it? You have no experience in the business, have you?" Somervell's reply was in the brisk Army manner: "I can't lay an egg, but I sure as hell can smell a rotten one."

Among present-day managers, no one considers himself more of a pro, nor takes more pride in his versatility, than Edward Harold Litchfield, a Ph.D. from the University of Michigan, who is now in his early forties. Even at so tender an age, Litchfield has already held down no fewer than eighteen jobs, and at last count was putting in time on half a dozen simultaneously. Among other things, he was chairman of Smith-Corona Marchant (typewriters and office machines). He was a director of Avco. He was a member of Studebaker-Packard's executive committee. He was chancellor of the University of Pittsburgh. Litchfield has run everything from government agencies to philanthropic organizations. He works eighty hours a week, and *Fortune* magazine has said that "he may be the busiest executive in the U.S."

To Dr. Litchfield, every job is the same. Whatever company or committee or government agency or charity he may be running at the time, he reasons, the same administrative techniques apply. To put it another way, Litchfield believes—like the American Management Association—that anyone who can run a jelly bean factory can just as easily run an electronics company.

But can he?

Many of the No. 1 men think that the jack-of-all-trades

theory of management makes about as much sense as concluding that a good swimming coach, ipso facto, would make a good football coach, as well. "I am not at all interested in the 'general' executive," says Owens-Illinois's chairman J. P. Levis—"the professional manager who can move from industry to industry. I would rather take the specialist who has stayed with one organization and train him as a general executive." And from Morgan Guaranty's chairman Henry Alexander come these words of doubt: "I'm not convinced that there's such a thing as the man who can perform with equal brilliance in any field; if he seems to, it may be only because he's fortunate enough in each case to be backed up by brilliant specialists."

Nowhere does the argument against the jack-of-all-trades wax hotter than at Ramo-Wooldridge, the ultra-scientific space-and-electronics outfit outside Los Angeles. There are those who think that Ramo-Wooldridge itself may one day feel the need for more business-trained people among its top men, but for the moment, at least, Simon Ramo and Dean Wooldridge have little use for the "professional" manager.

"The man who decides 'I am the leader type,' " says Ramo, "and takes courses in Advanced Heroism or Courage 100, often doesn't make out. The No. 1 mistake of management in this country is its preparation—or lack of it—for the scientific work ahead. Management tends to assume that the scientist needs an agent or a promoter who doesn't need to know anything about science, but that's wrong. If you're in the 'new-thing' business, the business of exploiting recent science, then there's an advantage in having managers who are 'new-thing' people. A manager from another business is not likely to be so successful; the man with a scientific background will always have an advantage here."

Ramo simply doesn't buy the idea of the professional manager. "The American Management Association," he says, "is plugging an unrealistic concept by describing management as a profession. It's true that the man who is good at management will be good with the management of various things. But the quarrel I have is that the concept of the professional manager overshadows the idea of expert knowledge of a business. The question is, *what* is he qualified to manage? Maybe he can go from a clothing company to a government job to an airline. But a general management type would find it a good deal harder moving into our business. In our business we don't sit back and relax with small changes in existing products. We're turning out new things."

Even such a skeptic as Ramo, however, would agree that a fundamental change has taken place in the manager's job and the training he must have to fill it. Less and less can the rising executive absorb all he needs to know, as he could in the past, by simple osmosis. More and more, as the body of managerial knowledge grows and the management job becomes more complex, he must be trained in the latest techniques.

This may not make him a journeyman manager. It may not even make him a good one. But it will at least give him a chance to battle among the heavyweights, where every fighter is a pro. "Management," says A.M.A.'s president Appley, "is now where the medical profession was when it decided that working in a drugstore was not sufficient training to become a doctor." Like doctors, executives have tended to become more and more specialized, but this, in turn, has put a premium on the general practitioner. The greater need for specialists, in short, creates a greater need for skilled general managers.

Thus it is that company after company, and college after college, have been offering courses for budding managers. And thus it is that companies ranging from Harvey's Hardware Store in Falmouth, Massachusetts, to giants like General Electric and du Pont, are willing to spare their key managers for weeks every year to study at the Astor or at another of A.M.A.'s postgraduate campuses (including the former Trudeau sanitarium at Lake Saranac, where corporate ills now are analyzed and treated with the same devotion that used to be lavished on tuberculosis patients). "Ten years ago," Appley recalls, "you could name on one hand the universities that had courses for business executives, and there were less than 10,000 executives enrolled in formal training courses either in their own companies or in universities. By now the figure has risen to 500,000 student-executives."

Since 1948, A.M.A.'s own membership has tripled, to 28,000, and its income now runs to $7.5 million a year, mostly from registration fees for its courses. From every state in the union, and from more than fifty foreign countries, some 70,000 executives come each year to take one or more of the 1,100 management courses A.M.A. has to offer, ranging from how to get new products flowing from the lab, to how to get old executives flowing into the ranks of the retired.

A good deal of this success no doubt is due to president Appley's own managerial prowess, and his hard-selling drive. It should be noted, however, that A.M.A.'s self-promotional techniques are not viewed with undiluted approval by all the men at the top. In the opinion of one New York executive, "It's a snow job. Once you pay your $50 membership fee, you're fighting your way out from under an avalanche of promotion material. They use the hard sell, and they also try to appeal to a sense of insecurity—the feeling that a guy is missing something really good if he doesn't sign up."

Some executives, who work for big companies, come away from A.M.A. courses feeling, as one said, that "it's 60 per cent stuff I already knew or could have figured out, 30 per cent sheer baloney, and 10 per cent usable new knowledge." And there are some who are skeptical of a certain pompous, do-gooder tone that here and there slips into A.M.A.'s preaching. (One three-page company "creed," cited in the basic management course, offers this ringing sentiment: "WE BELIEVE—That our Suppliers and their salesmen with their specialized knowledge of the products and services they sell, have played an important part in making Milton Roy the world leader in the design, manufacture and sale of controlled volume pumps.")

Nevertheless, when A.M.A. makes a convert—and it has converted thousands—the conversion sticks. It is a matter of changing a man's whole approach to his job, leading him to what Appley calls "the vital shift." Appley once described this moment of truth in an interview with *Management Methods* magazine: "Take an engineer, for example. He may have a management title and fifty engineers working for him, but every day his problems are engineering and he thinks of himself as an engineer. He will never make the shift until he gets away from the job for a week, or three weeks, or three months, goes somewhere and does nothing but *think* about the fact that he must drop his engineering specialty and become a manager of engineers. I have seen this take place—I have almost heard men's minds click when it suddenly dawned on them that 'I am no longer the best engineer in the world—I am trying to be the best engineering manager.'"

Lawrence Appley would be the last to claim that A.M.A. can make a manager out of any man simply by exposing him to a body of knowledge. "If he does not have the basic qualifications required," he says, "all the training and education in the world will not make him one." It is A.M.A.'s purpose to provide the place and the atmosphere in which the potential manager's mind can make the click.

When an executive attends an A.M.A. course, he is not taught by professors who got all their knowledge out of books, but by professional managers who have got religion (often from A.M.A. itself) and want to spread the gospel of professionalism to others by relating their own business experience. Appley likes to tell a story about a company for which he once worked. Years ago, he headed a committee to develop a new merchandising program for the company. "For this meeting," he says, "the company hid us away in a hotel in Albany. We weren't allowed to leave the hotel . . . not even our wives knew where we were. All of these precautions were taken because the company was afraid some competitor might get some of the information that we were exchanging among ourselves."

But times have changed. Recently one of the members of that committee, now a department head of the company, appeared before an A.M.A. meeting and passed around copies of a report that had the word "Confidential" written heavily across the top. The report told how his company had approached a certain problem, and solved it; everyone at the meeting was given a copy to take back to his own firm. "Obviously," says Appley, "the attitude of this company is that by giving out that material, and working with representatives of other companies, explaining how they had solved this particular problem, they, in turn, can expect to receive information from all of the companies represented in that room on how they solved certain of their problems. So if one company gives information on problem-solving to fifteen other companies, for example, that company can expect those fifteen others to give something in return. Obviously, by participating in A.M.A. a company gets more than it gives."

Foreign businessmen who have been exposed to this kind of American give-and-take find it nothing less than unbelievable. A few years ago, one instructor for the Committee for International Progress in Management went to Finland to conduct a seminar for a group of Finnish executives. For days, he tried to lure his businessmen-students into the discussion by asking them how they dealt with certain problems in their own companies. But every time he tried, he was greeted with stony silence. Finally, one morning, he took all the money they had paid for the course and laid it on the table before him. "Gentlemen," he said, "please come and collect your money. The only way you will get anything out of this seminar is to participate in it, and I can see that you are unwilling to do this. So I am giving you your money back." That broke the ice. The canny Finns began to exchange information on their operations, and were amazed to discover, as time went by, that they were not using their new knowledge to drive one another out of business.

The exchange of information within American business

is by no means limited to the classroom. Day after day executives of one steel company will tour the plants of another to inspect new production processes. And in Detroit, the information flows so freely—both by espionage and otherwise—that no automobile maker is ever in much doubt as to what his competitors are up to.

The idea of business being a profession is a new one. Half a century ago, the cognoscenti of Boston chuckled when President Lowell of Harvard, in composing a citation for the degree offered by Harvard's new Graduate School of Business Administration, described business as "the oldest of the arts and the youngest of the professions." It was not, as Frederick Lewis Allen pointed out years later in *The Big Change*, "simply because the language he used reminded people of the identity of the oldest of the professions. They thought the whole idea preposterous. Business, a profession! What an innocent notion! Business was a rough-and-tumble battle between men whose first concern was to look out for number one, and the very idea of professors being able to prepare men for it was nonsense. As a matter of fact, many a tough-fibered tycoon of those days was dubious even about employing college graduates."

Business is still the youngest of the professions, and it still is regarded by many with almost as much suspicion as the oldest, even though three-fourths of the American population is engaged in some form of business. The novelists have helped stoke the fires of skepticism, continuing to view the businessman as a boor, or a sharpie—or at best a dullard. "The businessman comes on stage," wrote Crawford Greenewalt in *The Uncommon Man*, "as an uncouth character who scoffs at all cultural pretensions and who will stop at nothing to fill his pockets. It's not a pleasant concept, and it is not any closer to the truth than our other stereotypes: The absent-minded professor, or the drunken reporter, the long-haired musician, the interfering mother-in-law, or the plumber who arrives without his tools."

But if the stereotype has not changed, the real-life businessman has. Today, more and more, he is a pro. This change has been marked by the birth of more than one hundred graduate business schools all over the country, dedicated like A.M.A. to the proposition that business is a a pursuit for professionals. Among these new institutions, none has done more to professionalize management than the Harvard Business School. In its day, it has turned out twenty-three thousand graduates and sent them into almost every field where a man can turn a profit—and many where he cannot. Among the unquestioned pros who have emerged from the Harvard Business School are president G. Keith Funston of the New York Stock Exchange, and the following presidents of corporations: Howard Joseph Morgens of Procter & Gamble; H. Gardiner Symonds of Tennessee Gas Transmission; Mark W. Cresap of Westinghouse Electric, and Edward J. Hanley of Allegheny-Ludlum Steel. The graduates of the class of 1949 already *average* $14,000 a year.

What has given Harvard its professional air, and produced its professionals, is a combination of teacher and teaching method. The Business School's professors belie the old bromide that those who can, do, and those who can't, teach. These men can, and they do, and they also teach. Many of them have had broad business experience;

many act as consultants to a roster of blue-chip firms. One such is Professor Myles M. Mace, who recently returned to the Business School after a stint as vice president of Litton Industries. Having had a close look at how things are done in the business world, Mace concludes that the job of the Business School is not to load its students with facts to be memorized, but "to help young men to learn how to think usefully about the solution of administrative problems."

To do this, the Business School, like a law school, uses the "case method" of instruction, in which actual business problems are presented for study, analysis and solution. "The whole system is decision oriented," says Mace. "There are no 'answers' to our problems. We can train people in marketing, finance, accounting, and so on, but the primary job is not to teach them a big body of generalities but to teach them how to think about making decisions on business problems."

Over the years, Harvard has compiled some twenty-five thousand "cases" for its students to discuss and try to resolve. The Ford Foundation's Donald K. David, who was dean of the Business School for years, estimates that, during his two years of training, a student may have to cope with as many as a thousand different business problems, ranging from the complicated financial affairs of the giant corporation to the human situations that may arise in any business at any time.

There is the case of Joan Leskoli; for instance—"a woman with many years' experience in a department store. [She] is verging on a complete mental breakdown. She should be dismissed, but dismissal may mean the final break." What to do?

Then there is the case of "The Boss is the Boss," wherein "a top manager puts pressure on one of his subordinates to promote a man other than the one the subordinate would have chosen." What should the junior man do?

And the case of Turen, Inc.—"a new firm (two men) producing a new product (pet door) is faced with the problem of pricing and marketing their product." Should they sell it through pet stores? Or supermarkets? Or by direct mail?

Harvard has no "Business School answer" for these or any other cases; as Professor Mace says, it is not in the business of teaching its students answers, but teaching them how to think.

When Harvard's Business School was founded in 1908, the first courses went straight down the industrial line—lumbering, printing, railroading, banking—but as the years have passed most of these courses have disappeared. The courses that have replaced them are at once a cause and an effect of management's changing view of itself and its functions. "Thirty years ago," says Professor George Albert Smith, "we instituted a course in business ethics. It was a fizzle. Now I can name three courses we would not have had twenty years ago that we have today: Human Relations, Business Responsibilities in the American Society, and Business, Society and the Individual."

What has a man got, once he has earned his M.B.A. at Harvard? One graduate says flatly: "The best business education available anywhere at any price." Almost any employer will agree that the kind of training Harvard gives amounts to a wealth of experience that most men could not accumulate in years of working at a job. The Business School graduate can expect to start at about $6,000 a year.

The only trouble with him, says an executive in a large chemical company, is that "it's sometimes hard to get him down from board-of-directors-level thinking, to working at the job he was hired to do."

A master's degree in business will almost surely give a young man a head start, but it can't keep him out front. Like every other hireling, particularly if he goes into a large corporation, the business school graduate must battle for recognition all the way. And the best way to get ahead, in the opinion of Harvard's former dean David, is to teach the man below how to get ahead. "You never get promoted when no one else knows your current job," says David. "The best basis for being advanced is to organize yourself out of every job you're put into. Most people are advanced because they're pushed up by the people underneath them rather than pulled up by the top."

This ability to develop people down the line is the hallmark of the truly professional manager. One after another, the top men of American business say that this is the most important part of their jobs. "A good manager," says Shell's president H. S. M. Burns, "is a man who isn't worried about his own career but rather the careers of those who work for him. My advice: Don't worry about yourself. Take care of those who work for you and you'll float to greatness on their achievements." Pittsburgh's Richard K. Mellon, who has a hand in controlling several of the nation's biggest companies, including Koppers, Gulf Oil and Alcoa, puts it simply: "It's all people."

But how to spot the people, when you are dealing with tens of thousands, and perhaps hundreds of thousands? This is a problem that bothers almost all the top men.

"We have a regular procedure," says M. J. Rathbone, the president of Standard Oil of New Jersey. "Every year, the manager of each affiliated company reviews his executive group right down to the engineering and technical level. The man is rated on personality, performance and potential for advancement by his direct superior and his department head. The outstanding ones in the rating are earmarked for the executive development program."

Even when a man has been tapped for such a course, however, there is a danger that he will be lost in the shuffle. I.B.M.'s Tom Watson, Jr., for one, is trying to prevent that from happening. Every month I.B.M. puts about fifteen of its brightest young executives through a company-run school, to give them an idea of what is going on in all the divisions of the corporation. In the past, Watson made a point of dining with each group as it went through, to have a look at the men, but he found it "pretty much of a hit or miss proposition." As a result, Watson recently decided on a different procedure. Now, he and three of his top men each spend half an hour or so interviewing every student who takes the course. It is a time-consuming process, but Watson thinks it will pay off. What does he look for among the comers? "Unusual drive plus a certain amount of diplomacy," he says. "If you can't direct the drive and harness it, it's useless. My father used to say that a good manager carries an olive branch in one hand and a baseball bat in the other, and is prepared to use either one at the right time."

To the baseball bat and the olive branch, du Pont's Crawford Greenewalt has added another managerial tool —the "skimmer chart." With this device, Greenewalt keeps an eye on all the up-and-coming executives among his eighty-five thousand employees.

Every one of the three thousand top-paid men in du Pont is plotted on a skimmer chart covering his department, according to his age and salary. At a glance, Greenewalt spots those men who are out-performing others in their age group, and promptly skims them off. "I'll sit down with the manager of a department and say, 'Tell me about Smith,'" Greenewalt explains. Since the vast majority of du Pont's managers can be found right in Wilmington, chances are that Greenewalt will already know the man, at least casually. If he wants to know him better, he will ask his boss to bring him along to the next executive committee luncheon. Or if there is a man, say, in Niagara Falls, who pops up above the line, Greenewalt will make an effort to meet him the next time he is in Niagara Falls—"without any hoo-rah."

Greenewalt is convinced that this system, combined with du Pont's decentralized operation, brings the pros to the top; and he is even more convinced that there have been few cases where a man's talents have been by-passed. "I would say that far more have been promoted who have not made the grade than have failed to reach positions within their capacity. In looking at promotions and advances over a long period of time, I think we've made more errors of commission than we have of omission."

# 7.

# THE

# EXECUTIVE

# FLESH MARKET

HOWEVER MANY SKIMMER charts, interviews and other techniques a company may employ to make sure that the right men rise to the top, there will always be some who don't get there fast enough—or who are blocked, through no fault of their own, by bad timing or bad luck of some other kind. Such a man was Henry Harden, executive vice president of American Window, Door & Sash.

At forty-five, Harden was making $100,000 a year and almost everyone in his town of 300,000 regarded him as a pillar of the community. But something was missing. In the first place, Harden's company offered no stock options, and even at his salary level he was unable to save any significant amount of money, certainly not enough to build an estate for his children. Secondly, Harden's old friend and colleague, Frank Johnson, had just been made president of the company. Johnson was only two years older than Harden. Obviously if Harden ever wanted to head a company himself—and he did—he would have to move on.

But how?

Like many another man in such a spot, Harden thought of the alternatives. He could let some of his friends know about his desire to move—but who among them could do anything for him? Or he could let the word slip out at the next industry convention—but then it was sure to get right back to his company even before he got home. Finally Harden decided to make out a résumé and ship it off to an acquaintance in New York, a man who specialized in finding executives for top jobs, and who had once approached Harden on such a man-hunting mission. But how to get the résumé typed? Harden didn't want his secretary to do the job, and he couldn't type himself. His wife could type, but he didn't want her to know that they might be moving, and thus upset the family prematurely and perhaps needlessly. He thought of using a public stenographer, but decided that if he did the word would surely get around town fast. Finally Harden hit on a solution: He would wait until his business next took him to Dallas, a thousand miles away; there, he felt, it would be safe to use a public stenographer.

At last, Harden sent off his résumé, and waited expectantly for employers to come knocking at his door. But at last report, months later, he was still working at American Window, Door & Sash.

The names in this story are fictitious, but the essential facts are true—and typical of the plight of many a top executive when he wants to switch jobs. For it is one of the paradoxes of the manager's life that, while there is a tremendous and growing demand for his talents, it is probably harder for him to find a job than it is for almost anyone else. It has been estimated that an executive switching jobs should allow himself a year to find a presidency, and six months to find a vice presidency.

Part of the trouble is the matter of timing; even the best of men can do nothing about it if the most likely jobs in their industry happen to have been filled just before they started looking. Then, as our window-and-door man discovered, there is the propriety involved: How to look around without causing a ruckus in the office. There is also the surprising fact that, as *Fortune* once said, "very few executives know how to go about selling themselves into a new position." They will make the same sort of gaffes as a fuzzy-cheeked college boy looking for his first job: they will be overanxious in an interview, or underinterested; they will wear the wrong clothes, say the wrong things, bring up the matter of money at the wrong time.

On top of all that, there is a reluctance on the part of many companies to hire from the outside, both from fear of damaging morale among their employees, and from fear that the new man won't work out. On the first point, chairman Stanley Allyn of National Cash Register says: "I think there is something wrong with the organization which has to go to the outside to fill top executive posts." On the second, president Thomas M. Evans of diversified H. K. Porter tells about a conversation he once had with Colonel Willard Rockwell, boss of Pittsburgh's Rockwell Manufacturing Co. (meters and machine tools). "When we hire three people and get one good man, we figure we're doing well," Evans told Rockwell. "Hell," answered the colonel, "you're boasting." President R. S. Reynolds, Jr., of Reynolds Metals adds: "I think that it is far better to develop the management personnel in your own company or own industry, rather than depend on professional outsiders or going out of the company to get managers. Only in exceptional cases should this be done."

There are, of course, a number of dissenters—as there are on every question posed to the No. 1 men. Not surprisingly, many of the dissenters are men who have done a good deal of moving around themselves. One of the dissidents is James J. Nance, who made a big reputation as the boss of General Electric's Hotpoint appliance division after World War II. Nance started with National Cash Register, moved to the Frigidaire division of General Motors, became a vice president of Zenith Radio and—after heading Hotpoint—successively became president of Packard and of Studebaker-Packard, and then a vice president of Ford. "I have never been a conformist to the prevailing pattern," Nance says. "I have always been independent, never placed a premium on security as most people do these days. When I went to Ford I wasn't identified as a Ford man; I was identified as Jim Nance." But in 1959, many months after he left Ford, Nance was still identified as Jim Nance; he hadn't yet found the right new job to step into.

Although many companies are wary of hiring top men on the outside, more and more have been doing just that, particularly since the Second World War. To those who engage in this kind of a manhunt, the practice is known variously as "cross-fertilizing," "recruiting," or "redistributing" executive talent. But to those who have it practiced on them, it is known as "ivory hunting," "pirating," "raiding," or outright "cannibalism." Whatever its proper name, the American Management Association has found, in a survey of fifteen hundred firms, that two out of five companies go to the outside to hire more than 10 per cent of their top talent, and 85 per cent of them do some of their top-talent hunting in other companies.

In some industries, notably steel, there is a great deal of circulation in the executive ranks. *Fortune* discovered that 60 per cent of steel's executives "have previously worked for two or more companies, 45 per cent for three or more, 30 per cent for four or more. More than half of the top steel executives were imported into their present companies as executives, and 44 per cent of them were imported when they were forty or older. Circulation is almost as intense in aircraft, in part because of the industry's newness. . . . This pattern is followed by many textile managers, and to a lesser degree by auto and auto-parts managers and metals managers."

In the practice of pirating, or raiding, or cross-fertilizing, the ethics are variable. Some companies say they won't talk to a man who already is working for someone else— unless he makes the first approach. Some won't talk to a man who is working for a competitor or a supplier without first warning his superior that they are casting a covetous eye in his direction. But it is a well-known fact that many man-hunting companies in such fast-growing fields as chemicals and electronics go out to raid their competitors with never a blush. One such company, A.M.A. reported, went so far as to circularize "every engineering executive in an older and larger firm, [and] hired a few at salaries the original employer didn't feel justified in paying."

One of the most successful manhunts of recent times was conducted by Henry Ford II after the war. He hired away executive vice president D. S. Harder from E. W. Bliss Co., where he had been president; he got chairman Ernest Breech from Bendix Aviation, where he had been president; and Breech, in turn, recruited a whole platoon of executives from General Motors, where he had worked before. In similar fashion, president George Spatta of Clark Equipment Co., the big road-machinery maker, has lured some of his top men from General Electric, where he used to work. "I'm a pirate," says Spatta straightforwardly.

The reason that the manhunt has stepped up of late can be found, in part, in the demand created by the growth and decentralization of old industries and the proliferation of new ones that have not had time to grow their own executives. Booz, Allen & Hamilton, a management-consultant firm, has estimated that industry is adding executives at a rate 46 per cent faster than prewar. Going back to those Depression days, one can find two more reasons for the shortage (or maldistribution) of executives today. For one thing, during the Depression, said New York Central's director of management development, "we just didn't replace anyone. There was no input at the bottom for about ten years"—and during the war there was hardly much more.

Then, too, there was the fluctuating birth rate. During the prosperous twenties, the birth rate was running at 25 per 1,000 population, but in the Depression thirties it slipped to 19 per 1,000 and stayed low during the war (it has since bounced back to 25 per 1,000 again). The result of this is that the most productive age group—from twenty-five to forty-four—has not been expanding as fast as have the less productive groups at either end of the wage scale. Thus, fewer people must produce—and manage the production—for more.

The search for capable managers has become so intense in recent years that a whole new breed of private eyes has

sprung up to do the job. These are the management recruiters, who spend every waking hour on the lookout for
the right man to fill the right job at the right time. Their
files are crammed with hundreds of thousands of executive biographies—often without the knowledge of the executives themselves. Does a company want a production
manager, or an advertising vice president, or a president?
The file cards flip, letters and discreet telephone calls go
out to various candidates. Interviews are held, references
checked, and finally the field is narrowed to the two or
three most likely men.

Some of the recuiters do their manhunting as a sideline
to their regular management consulting businesses—and
some of these men have themselves been snared in the
great manhunt. President John Burns of R.C.A., for example, was doing a consulting job for Radio Corporation as
a partner in Booz, Allen & Hamilton when he was hired
away by David Sarnoff. President Mark W. Cresap of
Westinghouse was doing a job for that company as a senior partner of Cresap, McCormick & Paget when Westinghouse tapped him for bigger things.

Among the score or so firms that do nothing but hunt for
top men, one of the best is New York's Ward Howell Associates. A Yale man who measures six feet six in his stocking feet, Ward Howell has a booming voice to match, and
has been on the prowl, on occasion, for such clients as
Continental Can, Celanese Corp., the Columbia Broadcasting System, American Motors and National Biscuit Co.
Like other recruiters, Howell is paid by the company that
is looking for the man, not by the man who is looking for
a job. If he fails in his search, he charges a fee of about .
$150 a day; if he finds the man, he usually collects about

20 per cent of the lucky executive's first-year compensation, plus expenses. Thus, placing a $50,000-a-year man can make the candle well worth the chase.

To fill a job for a client, the recruiters usually pick a man who is already employed; some of them scornfully refer to executives who write in or wander in off the street as "strays." But on the theory that the more men he has on file, the better are his chances of filling any job, Ward Howell welcomes the strays. In his files are hundreds of letters from men who have been passed by or think they are about to be. "I want more responsibility and greater prestige," one of them writes. "I want only one thing," writes another—"the presidency of a large company with stock options." A thirty-six-year-old says: "I'm netting over $50,000 a year, but oddly enough my interest flags without a constant goal just beyond reach. I find the load is too light." (In this particular case, the load consists of being president of not one, but two thriving small companies.)

One of the job seekers wrote candidly: "I'm making $100,000 this year, but I want more money. Obviously my motives are selfish, but there are too many young men today who are unwilling to take a step which means a gamble, afraid to try the unknown—what appears to be out of reach . . . I'm ready." Almost all express a high regard for their own ability. "My finest quality," wrote one, "is controlled aggressiveness." And another put his case this way: "To leave my present position, I do not feel that $50,000 would be sufficient. I'm worth $100,000."

In the Howell files, whole company stories come to life. Here lie the bodies—and the hopes—of no fewer than six top-level men who were axed out of one company by its ruthless boss. And here is the wreckage strewn at another company, an appliance maker, by its hard-bitten hatchet man. "I made as much as $260,000 with the X appliance company," one executive explains. "When the company was sold, I got out and landed as the number two man at Y. The job lasted less than six months. It was a basic policy disagreement." Another top man, tossed out of his job by a new management, has been in Howell's files for more than three years. In his heyday he was making more than $100,000. Now he's close to sixty years old, and very likely won't find another such job. Another man writes: "My top salary in my last job was $75,000. However, I'd be interested in anything over $30,000 now."

Some of the people who write in to Howell play it cozy, at first. One proper Bostonian wrote in his first letter: "I'm willing to listen, but please do not conclude that I will allow my name to be bandied about promiscuously as one seeking a connection." Howell then asked him to suggest someone for a job. The Bostonian, who had been president of an electronics company, replied: "At the moment I am unable to suggest a candidate other than myself. Two years ago, I resigned to relax and enjoy myself. After a trip abroad, I found a certain emptiness in not having a business association. . . ."

Such letter writers, like as not, will jump at the first reasonable opportunity offered. But in the vast majority of cases, the recruiters are trying to hire men already happily at work. Another of the top manhunters in New York is Sid Boyden, who with his staff is constantly at work trying to supply twenty-five to fifty top men for jobs ranging from $25,000 up. Boyden doesn't like to be called a recruiter. "You don't recruit a top executive," he says; "you recruit college kids. We use the word 'search.' We're an executive search firm." And sometimes the search is just the beginning. "In a high percentage of the men we move," Boyden explains, "the last thing they are thinking of is making a move. We have to create a degree of interest. That's part of the skill of negotiating."

Boyden outlines a typical assignment—to find a president for a $100 million manufacturing firm. "We find a man who looks like he qualifies because of his experience, other data, and the reputation of his present company. We pay him a visit in his office. Then, if we feel he is the caliber we are looking for, we try to figure out what would make him move. . . . Our job is to find out something about him from him directly—his compensation, pension arrangement, stock option plan, the age of his president—after all, that's a big factor in his possible advancement. We have to find out in what areas our offer should interest him."

First, he must have the urge—like Henry Harden of the window and door company—to be a president. If, like Harden, he is working for a young president, there is a good reason for him to move; and if, like Harden, he has no stock options and is offered some in the new job, he has another. "We now have strong motivation," says executive-hunter Boyden, "two solid reasons why he should move—the chance to be president and to build an estate. We know the qualities of the two companies. Say ours is expanding, his is not. The man is growing, but his company isn't. We appeal to his ambition, his desire for more challenging problems."

How long does it take for a recruiter to fill a job? From the day he sits down with a client and hears the job described, Boyden says, "par for the course is to recom-

mend one or two qualified men in sixty to ninety days."
The recruiters do not claim infallibility, but they do tend
to claim that when they fail it's somebody else's fault—and
very often, it is.

There is an astonishing list of taboos observed by different companies, both consciously and otherwise, and
when a man unwittingly runs into one of these, he can't
do much about it. Some bosses don't like bow ties; one will
not knowingly hire a top man who wears false teeth; another decided against hiring a man because of the way he
ate a piece of pie, beginning by cutting into the pointed
end (the prospective employer felt that any real individual
would attack the problem in some less orthodox manner).
Not long ago, Ward Howell ran into a company president
with a strong preference for Midwesterners, believing that
they are physically stronger than men produced by any
other part of the country.

In his book, *The Growth and Development of Executives,* Harvard's professor Myles Mace tells this story: "In
one company . . . the president has been personally in-
fluential in the hiring of 14 men during the last five years.
When he and 'his boys' get together, the assemblage resembles a team of professional football players; every man
is more than six feet in height and all have strong physical
characteristics. Inquiries as to the reasons for employing
various members of this group bring out many reasons,
none of which include physical stature and appearance.
Further discussion with other executives in the company,
however, disclosed that the president believes executives
are strong men, and, despite the proffered reasons for
employment, he unconsciously disqualifies any short or
slightly statured men, and requires that his men be big."

The recruiters recognize that it is management's prerogative to entertain such biases, and that often a candidate will be turned down for personal reasons. "The client may spend a weekend with the man," says Boyden, "then another with the man and his wife. He'll take him out and see how he acts on the golf course. He'll examine his family relations, really put him under a microscope. He has to. After all, the reason a president comes to us is that he is interested in having a confidential search made for a man who is going to be a member of his business family. The whole interviewing and negotiating period has to be most thorough, with nothing left to chance."

No matter how they may strive, however, the recruiters cannot eliminate chance altogether. A few years ago, Ward Howell filled an executive vice presidency for a restaurant chain. Months later, he got a call from the chain demanding its money back. "What happened?" asked Howell. "Didn't the man work out?" "No," said the client. "He dropped dead last week."

New York's Bertel Antell, who runs a smaller recruiting firm, remembers another man who didn't work out, because of his wife. She had been the belle of her home town in the South, and Antell warned her to curb her gregarious ways when she moved with her husband to his new job in an arch-conservative Indiana city. The warning was to no avail; no sooner had she arrived than she threw a party for her visiting grandmother, inviting the locals before she had set foot in any of their homes. The ensuing social freeze was so deep that the couple quit the job and the town in a matter of weeks.

The wife's role in the managerial life has long been a favorite subject for fiction writers. But few have handled it with quite the romanticism of a recent magazine short story. In the story, Cord Walker, rising young executive, is warned by his secretary that his wife is on a card file in Personnel—and what is said about her isn't good. She is, according to company records, just too exuberant. It happens that just then Cord and his exuberant lady are invited to the boss's house for dinner. Should he tell his wife about the card file, and get her into line? He decides not to.

Off they go to dinner with the boss and some other of the company's young executives. For a while, everything goes smoothly. But before long, Cord glances across the room and discovers, to his horror, that his wife has arranged herself cozily on the floor for this formal occasion. Always the lady, the boss's wife sits down on the floor beside her as the other guests look on aghast. But somehow, while realizing her social blunder, Cord's wife, Theo, carries the whole thing off, with head held high.

As the story closes, Cord is back in the office. Enter his secretary, slipping him Personnel's new information on his wife: "Obviously Theo Walker is alert and socially adaptable—and brave." At this, young Cord is almost overcome. As the story says: "He felt a swelling of pride, and knew the words were warm and true and that there was humanness in the man who had written them. He slipped the paper into his pocket and sat awhile in thought. He felt a surging sureness that some day he was going to be president of the company. He allowed the thought to wash over him and refresh him, and then a little laugh broke in his throat. Then, by George, everyone would sit on the floor. . . ."

Whether this is the goal of most men on their way up

the managerial slopes is open to question—but the matter of the wife's importance is not. Most of the country's top executives strongly believe that the wife can make or break a man's career, and many of them take pains to look over the wife these days when hiring an executive for a top-level job. This is particularly true when the job is one that will take the new man abroad or into a small community. "We think the wife is vital," says world-wide operator Edgar Kaiser. "Ours is a growing, demanding business; it's not a regular nine-to-five job, and if she doesn't understand, it's awfully hard on the man. Some of our people have left us, realizing that they can't travel and spend the time they'd like to with their families." When Kaiser is hiring a top man, he will arrange to meet the wife personally, sometimes by inviting her to his home for dinner.

Because of their widespread foreign operations, often in small communities, many oil and mining companies take a particularly close look at the wife before hiring a man. "The executive's wife can help her husband greatly," explains Socony Mobil's president Albert Nickerson, "if she easily adapts to new surroundings in foreign lands." And conversely, of course, she can do great damage if she doesn't. "We have several personal interviews with the wife," says Jersey Standard's M. J. Rathbone. "We try to appraise if they are the kind that can readapt themselves to foreign living. They have to have a little bit of pioneering spirit. We try to interest them in learning the foreign language, but the main thing we look for is emotional stability. If she's a whiner, thinks that foreigners are inferior, she can do a lot of harm. And they often have done harm. We've had to recall some men because of their wives. Even worse are the ones that don't come to the surface. They may go on for years doing damage overseas."

One Midwestern company, which once brought a wife into the office for an interview with her husband, quickly dropped the practice after the first unfortunate experience. The company president recalls: "This man's wife sat in the corner of my office knitting, while we got started talking; it was supposed to be sort of a symbol of her detachment, I guess. But every time I started to bear down on this guy, asking him why he held certain views—you know, testing his mettle—she would leap from her chair and come over to her husband and say, 'Charlie, you don't have to answer that question. I wouldn't let that man talk to you that way.' Needless to say, the poor guy didn't get the job."

Wives are only one of the many factors that make manhunting such an unpredictable pursuit for recruiters like Sid Boyden and Ward Howell. Sometimes they will find the right man for a job in the employer's own company, right under his nose. Sometimes, after searching for months, they will produce several men who they think are qualified, only to be told to go hunting some more. On one such occasion, when Howell was trying to find a successor for a company president, he finally quit the chase, telling the president in exasperation: "I don't think you *want* me to find a man to succeed you." Another time, directors of an oil company wanted to hire a vice president to set up some competition for another man who was the heir apparent. But by the time the job hunt was completed, the heir apparent had so impressed the board that they decided not to hire a competitor after all; they went right ahead and made the first man president.

The manhunters can make or break a community, as well as an individual executive. Boyden tells of the time he was asked to find a top man for a firm in a town of ten thousand. "The company had a payroll of two thousand and was losing $500,000 a month. The whole town was affected. The grocery store credit files were bulging, the relief rolls were rising. We located a man. In one year, he had the company breaking even. At the end of the second year, it was making an acceptable profit. The credit files disappeared, the relief rolls dropped."

The executive scouts are accused, on occasion, of robbing Peter to pay Paul—and themselves. What is their answer?

Boyden, for one, offers this: "The strength of this country today is in the strength of its industrial economy. The strength of the economy is in direct ratio to the quality of top executives. The more qualified our top executives, the faster the economy grows. Any big business can buy a machine or an accounting system. It can buy a plant, hire employees, buy raw materials and hire ad agencies—and still the company will not grow if it doesn't have top executives. I believe every time Boyden Associates finds a man stymied in his job and moves him, we have directly contributed to the strength of the country. If we could go out and find all the men who are not working up to fullest capacity, who are ready for more responsibility, and move them into jobs where they could use all their talents, we'd really accomplish something. Put it this way: If our top executive talent in general is operating at 70 per cent of capacity, our economy is only operating at 70 per cent, too."

# MEN AT
# WORK

Boss: *Where's my pencil?*
SECRETARY: *Behind your ear.*
Boss: *Damn it, woman, I'm a busy man. Which ear?*

CRAWFORD GREENEWALT remembers exactly when the awful realization dawned on him. It was soon after he had been elected president of du Pont, and he was on his way to Washington to address the National Press Club. "There I was on the train with my speech clutched in my hand," he says. "Suddenly I thought, 'Dear God, what they think of the du Pont company depends on what they think of me.' I was petrified at the thought. Suddenly you wake up to the fact that even on a plant visit people are wondering what the hell kind of a guy this is. You're always on parade."

The business of being always on parade does not bother many of the No. 1 men (Greenewalt included, by now). But the resultant demands on their time can be overwhelming. Almost from the moment they wake up in the morning to the moment they close their eyes at night, they are badgered by swarms of people who want something of them—dealers demanding fast delivery, distributors demanding bigger margins, suppliers demanding higher prices, customers demanding lower prices, security analysts demanding information, charity leaders demanding money, to name just a few.

Bell & Howell's president Percy, who has devoted a good part of the past few years to streamlining his presidential job, once painted this picture of the harried managerial day, as he used to find it:

"The morning mail includes a request from the Chamber of Commerce for a speech on foreign trade, from a public service radio program for a talk on aid to education, from a service club for a talk on 'The Social Responsibilities of the Industrialist.' A shareowner writes for information on dividend policy; a security analyst asks about anticipated earnings. A group of teachers wants to tour the plant and exchange ideas with company executives.

"The phone rings steadily. A distributor in Holland calls about a new Trade Fair. An irate customer can't get service in Mule Shoe, Texas. A key dealer calls frantically about a fair trade violation.

"More mail: A distributor from Thailand announces an impending visit. A key dealer suggests cooperative advertising . . . 'but keep up your full schedule of national advertising.'

"Meetings: A civic lunch for Project B (the host had come to your luncheon for Project A). Back to the plant for a Budget Board meeting. Review a new product release. Turn down gracefully (impossible!) a request to introduce a friend to the Director of Purchases; discuss two new appointments in the Manufacturing Division and a major capital equipment acquisition. Write a column (due yesterday) for the employee newspaper.

"End of the day. Into the brief case goes the balance of the day's mail (or yesterday's) along with reading matter marked 'must.'"

This race against the clock is made necessary by the fact that the head of a company must keep up a cheerful public relations front, and appear to have time for almost anything that may come up or anyone who may drop by. "Either you're an s.o.b. for not seeing them," says a top tobacco man, "or you don't have enough time to do your job right." General Motors' chairman Donner complains: "My middle name is beck and call."

For the top men, there is no such thing as a typical day. Monday there may be a board meeting, Tuesday an inspection of a plant a thousand miles away, Wednesday an industry convention somewhere else. And just as the boss is thinking that Thursday will give him a chance to catch up in the home office, something will call him out of town again. Not long ago, Donner left his New York apartment one morning with a clear idea of just what he was going to do that day, starting with a physical exam from 9 to 10 A.M. But when he got to the office after the physical, "I found a telegram from Washington inviting General Motors to testify at hearings on a proposed new bill. So I was forced to fly to Detroit to work out the details"—whether or not G.M. should testify, and if so, who should say what.

The result of this kind of pressure, of course, is long hours of overtime. The Young Presidents' Organization recently polled its members and found that they average fifty-three hours a week at work—not counting the time spent at home over a bulging brief case; many top executives put in sixty-two hours a week, and more.

Still, the week isn't long enough. To make each hour measure more than sixty minutes, the men at the top have worked out a series of time-saving techniques—ways to cut meetings short, and otherwise to lighten the load. Time-consuming committee meetings present two seemingly contradictory problems: First, how to get people to talk, and second, how to shut them up. On the first, a number of top men have been using what Harold B. Schmidhauser of the American Management Association dubbed the "psychological minute"—a full minute of self-imposed silence after asking a question or stating a problem. Sixty seconds of quiet can seem like an eternity to the man who is running the meeting, but before the time is up someone is bound to begin talking and suggesting ideas, if only to break the embarrassing silence.

But how to shut them up? This is of even more concern to the man whose time is his most valuable possession. Of this problem, former vice president Leland Hazard of Pittsburgh Plate Glass says: "The moment I find myself not listening carefully to the other person, I know it's time for me to take over. . . . The trick is to remain silent in the early stages of a meeting, but you can't wait too long. It's picking that moment when the articulate ones have had their say and the inarticulate ones have not yet made up their minds. In every conference there comes a moment when those who have not thought the matter out in advance will hesitate. In that moment, if you know what you want to do, do it."

Different men have different approaches to the matter

of saving time. Some will seize any and every opportunity to dash off some dictation—in their cars or planes or homes —believing that this is the high road to efficiency; others will not dictate at all, believing that it is a useless waste of time. Samuel S. Auchincloss, head of Tracerlab, says that "when I dictate I feel I say *too* much, *too* often (and so do a lot of people, in my opinion)." Chairman Eugene Holman of Standard Oil of New Jersey will dictate only "a very few letters, and only the briefest of memos. Staff people do most of the letter writing and the preparation of memos as well as the lengthy and burdensome reading." Similarly, president S. Clark Beise of the Bank of America avoids as much reading as possible; he will often skip to the last page of a report, to see what's being done.

One of the most time-consuming, if gratifying, trends of recent years has been the development of increasingly good manners among America's top men of business. There may have been a day when the top executive greeted visitors with a quick handshake from behind his desk, and a wave to a nearby chair. But no more. The standard technique now is for the boss to come out to meet a caller, and usher him politely into his office. Chances are, the room resembles a living room more than an office, with the work area at one end and the talk area, complete with upholstered sofa and easy chairs and perhaps a wood-burning fireplace, at the other.

The front office décor is as varied as the No. 1 men themselves. Columbia Broadcasting System's chairman William S. Paley combines his love for art with his love for C.B.S. On the walls of his office high above New York's Madison Avenue hang sketches and paintings by such artists as

Rouault, Picasso, Watteau and Toulouse-Lautrec; but one side of the room is decorated entirely with ancient microphones bearing the call letters of C.B.S. radio stations. To decorate his office on Broadway, G.M.'s Donner chose a young master: Holding the place of honor on the chairman's wall is a misty harbor scene, painted by his son. Lever Brothers' former boss, architect Charles Luckman, uses his soft green Los Angeles office as a fine showplace to display his collection of antique brass mortars and pestles, brass figurines and other ornaments. Luckman, incidentally, works at what may be the most unusual desk in the country—an old rosewood piano, bleached and remodeled, whose massive legs sink ankle-deep into the rug.

A few of the top executives have done away with the desk altogether, using a coffee table and a telephone stand instead. Many sit at a plain table, with not a paper in sight (chairman Frank Pace of General Dynamics even keeps his telephone tucked away in a drawer). "If you put a desk between you and the other fellow," Pittsburgh Plate Glass's Leland Hazard once explained, "he feels your business is in the desk. But if you have just a table, he feels your business is with him." (Not surprisingly, Hazard used a slab of Pittsburgh plate glass for his table.)

The trouble with this kind of gracious office living is that it puts the caller into such a relaxed mood that he tends to sit around, passing the time of day and wasting the time of the boss. But there are ways to keep the flow moving. Edgar Row, vice president of Chrysler, used to keep his office temperature at a cool 55 degrees to discourage any loitering. The Glidden Co.'s president Dwight Joyce has a five-minute rule, which he often invokes: After a visitor's time is up, Joyce's secretary will come in to remind him of another appointment. Just as effective, if not quite so urbane, was the technique used by K. T. Keller when he ran the affairs of Chrysler. Whenever Keller found visitors tiresome, "I just told them they didn't have enough facts to interest me and suggested they return when they did."

Because of the endless stream of visitors, telephone calls, and other bothersome interruptions in the office, many of the top men actually welcome travel; it gives them a chance to catch up on their business reading and other matters they may have let slip—and it gives them time to think. Owens-Illinois's chairman J. P. Levis, who spends about a quarter of his time traveling, says: "I find that much more constructive work can be done away from my home office than in it. When I am traveling, I find that I have a much better perspective of the business and more opportunity to think about it and observe it."

There was a story that made the rounds a few years ago about a top executive who returned from an extended business trip in Mexico. When he got home, he dashed into his little son's room and threw open his arms for the grand reunion. The child just stared at him, without a flicker of recognition. "If you go to Mexico," he said blankly, "you can see my daddy." The story may be apocryphal, but in view of the amount of traveling the No. 1 men do in the course of a year, it is not impossible. Forty thousand miles is the figure for United Aircraft's chairman H. Mansfield Horner; 100,000 miles for General Electric's president Robert Paxton, a figure matched by Textron's Royal Little. Blaw-Knox president W. Cordes Snyder Jr. racks up the equivalent of five times around the world.

As might be expected, one of the most far-ranging travelers is world-wide builder Edgar Kaiser, who thinks nothing of popping off to Australia one week, and India the next. "I'm a trouble-shooter," says Kaiser. "I go where there's a problem and something's got to be done." In one recent twelve-month period, there were so many problems that Kaiser made no fewer than thirteen overseas trips. He went five times to Australia, twice to England and once each to India, Ghana and Iran, to name a few.

But as General Telephone & Electronics' chairman Donald Power points out, the nature of a top man's job is such that it shouldn't really matter where he is at any given moment; he can work just as effectively wherever he happens to be. J. P. Levis quite agrees: "Some of the most constructive ideas that one gets can be while shaving, or visiting with people socially, or even in the duck blind or on the fishing stream. To put it briefly, a business executive's mind is never far off from his business problems."

A few chapters back, we looked in on Cleveland's Dwight Joyce, getting up every morning at five-thirty and spending two hours thinking about himself, his business, and the world. Joyce may feel alone in those early-morning hours, but all over the country he could find company among other men at the top. Litton Industries' Tex Thornton often is up at five, and sometimes at four. (Working as he does on the West Coast, he is sometimes on the phone to New York by six.) In his home outside Chicago, Illinois Central's president Wayne Johnston is up every morning at five-thirty or earlier. One day not long ago, worrying over what to do about his executives' salaries for the next year, Johnston got up at four, went into the study adjoining his bedroom and spent two hours figuring it all out while his wife slept on. Johnston has breakfast every morning at six-fifteen, walks to the station (he has it clocked at exactly fourteen minutes), and is in his office downtown by seven-thirty.

No one is a more dedicated member of the dawn patrol than Mills Lane, the off-beat banker from Atlanta. "I get up at 5 A.M. every day," he says. "I smoke a pack of cigarettes and drink a pot of coffee—and I muse. If I ain't got a project to think about I'm not happy." Lane's projects range from new homes for children suffering from cerebral palsy (his own daughter is a victim of the disease), to a new investment club he recently set up for three of his friends—the manager and the cook of Atlanta's posh Piedmont Driving Club, and a local cop. One December morning, Lane got to thinking it would be nice to draw up a family genealogy and give it to his "kinfolk" for Christmas. But the list grew so long he never finished. He waves a sheaf of papers and says: "Look at all my goddamn kinfolk! Twenty pages of 'em!"

But mostly, when Lane muses in the early-morning hours, he thinks about his Citizens & Southern Bank. "I take a statement of condition and spread it out in front of me," he says, "and when I look at those figures I can see every department and every person in the bank. I just let my mind wander."

What does the top man's job really consist of?

"No one man, or two or three men," says Sinclair Oil's chairman P. C. Spencer, "can possibly know and run an enterprise as large as ours." Thus, the boss has to select certain functions and concentrate on them. Some managers, like Edgar Kaiser, consider themselves trouble-shooters. Atlanta retailer Richard Rich, for example, thinks that "top management should free itself and devote its time to 'exception' management. Don't pay attention to what's running right, but to what isn't running right." In the same way, C.B.S. chairman William Paley says: "I don't look at television shows that are out of trouble."

To keep himself on the right track, I.B.M.'s Tom Watson keeps a list of things that he should be concentrating on, and glances at it from time to time during the day. The list can range from the smallest detail to the broadest company policy. On the Watson docket recently, for example, was a note reminding him: " 'Will' in staff memos." (Watson had discovered that too many of the memos sent out by his staff officers to I.B.M.'s operating divisions included the command, "you will." The staff is supposed to advise, not command.) On the same day, there was listed a matter of long-range company policy: "Product development in Europe." ("Everything developed in our European plants," Watson explained, "seems to get pooh-poohed here, and if it goes on like this our European inventors are likely to get fed up and quit. They blame what they call an attitude of 'N.I.H.'—not invented here—so we've given them four or five small machines to develop on their own.")

Most of the top men believe that their real job is to plan for the future, to get their organizations on a path that will keep them profitable and dynamic five, ten or twenty years from now. At first, says Erik Jonsson of Texas Instruments, "I think I wanted to prove myself. Then I got to institution building." General Electric's Ralph Cordiner likes to say that half his time is spent making decisions that won't take effect until after he is retired.

Among the men who seem to have licked the problem of delegating responsibility, perhaps the champion is president R. L. Minckler of General Petroleum in Los Angeles. "It used to be that all you saw of him were the bottoms of his feet, he was on the go so much," a friend recalls.

"But now you can walk into his office at any time and find him with time on his hands." Minckler made three rules for himself: (1) Every night before he leaves the office, he writes down what he did that day that he will never have to do again—in other words, he lists the things he has now trained someone else to do; (2) he will never allow anything to be put on his calendar that *must* be done on a given day; and (3) he will never allow an emergency to arise that demands his presence. In the event of an earthquake or fire or some other disaster, Minckler knows that there are capable men who can handle the problem without him. He knows, because in planning for the future he has trained them to do so.

Someone once said that the real test of delegation is for a manager to watch another man do something he thinks is wrong and not say anything about it; yet not every top executive has the kind of self-discipline required to sit back silently and watch. One after another, the bosses insist that they reserve to themselves only the decisions involving top policy, long-range planning and personnel. But since it is up to them to decide where operations end and policy begins, the line is sometimes flexible to the point of being nonexistent. It might be argued, in fact, that one of the functions the top executive should delegate is the job of deciding just where this line should be drawn.

There is a case in point in the story of an oil company which decided a few years ago to change the corporate symbol on its filling stations, believing that the signs then being used were too drab and old-fashioned. The top man in the company named a three-man committee to select a new sign.

First the committee tested a series of shapes on a panel of fifty consumers, to see which was best remembered. The winner was a trapezoid. Then the committee hired a color expert to work out a combination of shades with a tested "come hither" look. Next, there was the matter of a symbol. Should the company try to create an image, as some thought, of a "friendly" firm? Or was its corporate image already too folksy, as others believed? At length, a symbol was chosen, the sign was put together, and testing began at filling stations in a number of key cities. The results seemed favorable, but months passed and nothing was decided. The reason was that the president of the company, who insists that he concerns himself only with "over-all policy matters," simply did not like the sign.

In the business of selling gasoline, it may be that such details are all-important. Certainly it is true in a service industry like transportation. President Donald Nyrop of Northwest Airlines, who gets to his St. Paul office every day at seven-thirty, described to a visitor last year the kind of problems he has to deal with in the course of a day. They can range from new financing and labor relations to the smallest details of aircraft décor. "Yesterday," he said, "we had to decide on the interiors that will go into our new Electras and DC-8 jets." Nyrop moved to a table behind his desk and proudly showed off a stack of nylon fabrics, fondling the material that had been selected. "The finest you can buy," he said. American Airlines' president C. R. Smith keeps an equally sharp eye on the details of his operation, forever showing up unannounced to test the food and service on American flights.

Certain things simply cannot and should not be delegated, of course. One of these, in the opinion of Shell Oil's president H. S. M. Burns, is worry. If he is doing a good job, the boss cannot help being keyed up, says Burns, who developed an ulcer for his labors. There are the TV appearances, the interviews, the congressional hearings, the constant traveling. "Many of my friends try to avoid this kind of thing," says Burns. "You can't. It's part of your job. I tell them, don't avoid congressional investigations, don't send your lawyer, insist on going yourself. I fought a war of nerves with Kefauver for three days, and I won. An executive is a guy with ulcers. Work doesn't do it—he can delegate that. It's overworry, not overwork." As a sign on the desk of Harry Truman used to say: "The buck ends here."

Not that the top men worry about every decision they have to make; they simply haven't time. But when they make a mistake, they quickly try to compensate for it. The decisions that *do* worry the managers are those that have to do with people. "If it were just a physical matter it would be easy," says Harllee Branch, Jr., of the Southern Co. "But the human aspect is what drives you nuts. There's no absolute right or wrong; and you've got that horrible problem of a man's family—the innocent bystanders."

What to do about the long-time, trusted employee who has started to drink? Should he be fired? If so, what about his wife and children? And is Jones the man to replace him, or should Smith get the nod? "When you make a mistake with a person," says banker Mills Lane, "there ain't no reserve you can charge it off against, and you can't forget it." In particular Lane cannot forget one individual whom he pushed too far too fast. The man didn't measure up to the responsibilities of his new job. He began to drink, and ended in a sanitarium. Was this Lane's fault? Lane thinks so. "I let him fly higher than he could roost," he says ruefully.

This painful aspect of the top management job bothers

even the toughest of the No. 1 men. "If you don't have some sentiment," says Litton Industries' Tex Thornton, "business becomes too coldly realistic. But you can't let sentiment dominate. Sometimes, for cripe's sake, you've just got to cut."

Such a cut had to be made some years ago in one large company, for a rather unusual reason. The firm was having trouble with a major department. A number of the key men were quitting, and the company was losing its historical share of the market as a result. When the president inspected, he found the reason: The department head was a homosexual. He was fired immediately, but it was years before the company got that key department built up again.

Many of the men at the top have spent years as operating men, and think they will miss the excitement of getting things done themselves when they switch to the job of getting others to do things for them. Yet they soon discover that however worrisome the human problems may be, it is in this area that they find their deepest sense of achievement. And while they sometimes get the feeling that the clock is gaining on them—or they can't remember which ear their pencil is behind—they love the race.

Sitting behind a table-desk in his office in Burbank, Lockheed's intense chairman Robert Gross drums his fingers on the window sill, fidgets with a paper clip, and says: "I'm amazed at the intensity with which we've all been working. The competition gets more and more intense. This business is changing so fast that we're all out struggling harder than ever before." But Gross has no desire to give up the struggle; he hasn't the faintest idea what he would do if he had to.

Few men are farther apart, in manner, than Gross and General Motors' seemingly placid chairman Donner. Yet deep down, Donner seems to have the same sort of enthusiasm. He thinks about his job for a moment, swiveling full circle in the chair behind his desk. "Business is a little like a battle," says Donner, who has made a hobby of reading up on the battles of the Civil War. "It's chaotic when you're in the midst of it. What most historians miss is the fact that battles are not fought through on any particular pattern."

It is this lack of pattern, this variety, this unpredictability, that makes business *fun* for the No. 1 men. "I'd be unhappy as hell if I didn't do this," says Edgar Kaiser of his taxing, travel-heavy job. "I *like* what I do!" And it is precisely the same sense of ever-changing fun and excitement that makes it so hard for the men at the top to call it quits and retire.

True, there are a number who expect to be fully prepared to step down when retirement age rolls around. Ralph Cordiner, for example, has been planning for the day: "I've been building a diversified cattle ranch on the West Coast of Florida. I hope this will prove so intriguing —and I think it will—that I won't want to come back." Cordiner, who turned fifty-nine in 1959, wants to retire before he is sixty-five—just as G.E.'s former chairman Philip Reed did before him. "The saddest thing is when a man tries to keep up interest in his old job after he retires," Cordiner says. "That's why I want to be fifteen hundred miles away." At fifty-four Chrysler's Tex Colbert says he looks forward to traveling and renewing old friendships that have dropped by the wayside during his busy life.

But most of the top men think of retirement, if they think

of it at all, with a sense of foreboding; for many of them, retiring from business would be the same as retiring from life itself. "I just can't imagine what I would do retired," says United Aircraft's H. M. Horner, now fifty-six. Nor can Lockheed's Robert Gross, who tells himself, but does not convince himself, that there are some things he would like to do: "I'd like to enjoy some of the things I haven't been able to. I've never spent any money, really. I'd like to have a boat, a couple of new cars, maybe build a new house or two." Then he admits: "I don't have much to turn to when I retire." What would happen to Lockheed if Gross retired tomorrow? "This place could get along without me, but I know that I'm the one person who has been driving for diversification and expansion. I think that if I gave up work this afternoon this program of reaching out into new fields might not go ahead as aggressively. This is my baby; I like to battle for it."

The No. 1 men echo one another on the subject of retirement. "I am not waiting to retire," says seventy-one-year-old hotelman Conrad Hilton. "When the time comes, I will keep on working." Railroader Wayne Johnston, sixty-one: "I deplore the idea of retirement." National Gypsum's Melvin H. Baker, seventy-four: "This business is my life. I have no intention of retiring in the foreseeable future." Clark Equipment's George Spatta, sixty-six: "I have a life contract with my company. I will never retire."

For many who, unlike Spatta, do not have such a contract, directorships have served as a helpful transition into retirement; but the business of switching from an operating job to an advisory function calls for a large measure of self-discipline. The board of Pacific Gas & Electric asked James Black to stay on as chief executive officer after he reached sixty-five, but he turned them down on the ground that "people down the line want me to get the hell out." Instead, Black agreed to stay on as chairman, with no executive authority. He thinks it has worked out fine, and that he has managed to "keep out of management's hair, but you've got to discipline yourself to beat the band." (Black also serves on a number of other boards, and is called on to do a number of "spot" jobs in Washington from time to time.)

Some executives move into consulting when they reach retirement age; others launch whole new careers. William E. Mitchell, former president of Georgia Power, was happily ensconced as president of the $7 million Atlanta Realty Co. when he turned seventy-five. "A retired man," he said, "should find some other interest to keep him busy so he won't go looking for a rocking chair." Sam Goldwyn, still hard at work at seventy-six, put it another way: "I find the longer you work, the longer you live."

Probably the two most notable proofs of this truism are Frederick H. Ecker, who at ninety-one was still putting in a good deal of his time as honorary chairman of Metropolitan Life; and Alcoa's former boss Arthur Vining Davis, who at ninety-one was in the midst of building up a new and diversified empire in Florida, ranging from real estate and resorts to ice cream and transportation.

With the average life span lengthening, a good deal more thought has been given, of late, to the problems of retirement. The labor unions have fought for, and in large measure won, the worker's right to a pension over and above the Social Security benefits he has paid for during his productive years. Retirement benefits of a financial nature have long been an established reward of executive work. What seems to be needed now, in view of the loudly bemoaned shortage of executive and directorial talent, is a way to retain the services and talents of industry's key men past retirement, without damping down the enthusiasm of the young bloods on their way to the top.

# 9.

## HOME WAS
## NEVER
## LIKE THIS

Some people work better in the morning, others at night; Harllee Branch of the Southern Co. is a late-afternoon man. He builds up steam as the day goes along, and hits his peak efficiency when most of his corporate colleagues are packing their brief cases and heading home.

The result of this end-of-the-day push is that by the time Branch gets home he has worked himself into a state of exhaustion. Often, he just puts on his pajamas, flops on his bed and watches TV while his wife, Kitty, brings him dinner in bed. Then, just as often, he will snap open his brief case and start catching up on matters that he wasn't able to get around to during the day at the office.

A former lawyer, Branch calls his family of four children "quite a little corporation," and refers to his wife admiringly as "my senior partner." "My wife is a very placid, undisturbed person with perspective," he says. "She has no capacity for serious criticism. She never undertakes to make a decision for me; she never calls me up at the office or interferes. She knows more people in the electric business than I do. She never gets upset when things are going bad and never gets overexcited when they're going good." Branch has some strong views on how much good such a woman can do a man. "I never saw a self-made man who didn't outmarry himself," he says. "You'll find that his wife is a better woman than he is a man. What my wife gave me made me hirable."

If other men at the top are not quite as vocal as Branch on the subject of their wives, it may be because few of them get the supper-in-bed treatment that Branch enjoys. But that is only part of the explanation. The plain fact is that, in many cases, the No. 1 men belong to their businesses first, to their wives and children second—and often the women and children are a very poor second, indeed. It takes but little imagination to reconstruct the conversations that sometimes take place between some of the top executives and their wives:

"But I promised the children we'd all go to the country this weekend."

"Sorry, dear, but something has come up at the Chicago plant."

"But I told the Joneses we'd go to the opera with them Thursday night."

"Sorry, dear, but that's the night I'm seeing Smith about the new merger."

"But I said that on Monday . . ."

"Sorry, dear."

When they think about it, many bosses are a little ashamed of how much time they devote to business. "My wife thinks I'm a little bit dizzy and daffy," says Lockheed's chairman Gross. "I guess people are critical of me for being so absorbed in my business. And maybe this makes me an unattractive person.\* I'm ashamed to say I've allowed my commercial life to dominate my personal life too much. I don't relax enough. I really want to relax. Sometimes I think, the hell with it, today I'll just go down to our beach house and skip the office. But I never do."

Whether or not they want it that way—and the suspicion is that many of them do—the job never stops. "Business dominates your whole life," says Goodyear Tire & Rubber's chairman E. J. Thomas. "Time with the family suffers terribly." The Bank of America's president Beise complains that "three or four nights a week, all or part of the evening is devoted to business, quasi-business, public or charitable gatherings." And banker Henry Alexander finds that he can count on "no more than one or two evenings quietly at home during a week."

The line between social and business entertaining has become so blurred for many that it is almost indistinguishable. There may be a dinner party, supposedly a social affair; but the conversation soon turns to business, and the managerial mind begins to whir.

Even on those rare evenings alone at home, business is no further away than the telephone. The phone will ring; it is the executive vice president with some pressing problem. President Ralph Burger of the Great Atlantic & Pacific Tea Co. puts it this way: "Even when we don't take work home, it has a tendency to follow us home."

For C.B.S.'s William S. Paley, the job is right there in his Long Island living room, staring him in the face with a twenty-four-inch gaze. He watches television an average

---

\* It doesn't.—O.E.

of two hours a night, often tuning in to both CBS and another channel simultaneously on a twin-screen set that makes him one of the few people in the country who can take in two ancient movies at one and the same time. Watching television, of course, is not exactly a form of relaxation for Paley. "I probably express more exasperation at what happens on TV than anyone else in the country," he says. What happens when Paley sees a CBS show that exasperates him? "Memoranda start to fly, hell is raised, meetings are held, people are blasted, and sometimes the show is dropped."

The job even follows the No. 1 men to bed. Years ago, the first John D. Rockefeller used to talk to his pillow, going over and over his business problems, telling himself "not to get puffed up with any foolish notion," warning himself to "look out or you will lose your head—go steady." Rockefeller told an interviewer: "How often I had not an unbroken night's sleep, worrying about how it was all coming out. . . . Work by day and worry by night, week in and week out, month after month."

It is not too different for many today. U.S. Steel's Roger Blough, Chrysler's Tex Colbert, Matson's Randolph Sevier, are all among the many men at the top who keep pad and pencil on their bedside tables, to jot down brainstorms that may break in the middle of the night. Sevier usually arrives at the office in the morning with his pockets stuffed with notes. "You may pop out of bed at 3 A.M. with the right idea," says Chevrolet's Edward Cole. One morning, Cole was surprised to hear his wife ask him: "What's a bell housing, dear?" (It is a bell-shaped covering for a piece of machinery.) When Cole inquired where she had ever heard the expression, Mrs. Cole replied: "Why, that's all you were talking about all night in your sleep."

A few of the bosses boast that they actually are able to forget about business at home. "To be perfectly frank," says United Aircraft's H. M. Horner, "when I get home at six o'clock at night I have a couple of real dry martinis and am then pretty well able to forget about the shop and take an interest in the home, such as the fact that the maid didn't properly dust the desk." But after he has done the proper amount of clucking over the dusty state of the furniture, Horner will turn to his reading for the evening— "and most of my home reading is on aviation plus news magazines and newspapers."

Like Horner, the vast majority of bosses do not have, or do not make time for much reading beyond the papers, the news and trade magazines, and reports or articles relating to their business. Roger Blough reported not long ago that he hadn't read a novel in years (an amateur cook, Blough used to keep a copy of *The Bed-Book of Eating and Drinking* on the table by his bed). Allegheny Ludlum's president Edward Hanley was inspired to read *Day of Infamy* as a result of a trip to Honolulu last year; it was the first book he'd read in six months. Not surprisingly, financial operator Louis Wolfson, the head of Merritt-Chapman & Scott, is "particularly interested in biographies of businessmen who have left their mark, for one reason or another, on our history. Occasionally, I find a book which holds my interest so completely that I will read it over many times—*The Age of the Moguls* being an outstanding example."

But there are those who do manage to carve out time to broaden their horizons, making a point of reading books far afield from their business. Oilman George Getty, for one, spends some of his time reading classical poetry. For another, president Raymond Stevens of Arthur D. Little, Inc., the Cambridge industrial research firm, says: "I read, intentionally, a wide variety of literature, history, and—as an anaesthetic—mysteries, etc., in modest percentage." Harry Bullis, while still active as chairman of General Mills, tried to read a good book every month. And Merck's John Connor read *Dr. Zhivago* and *Brave New World Revisited* alternately. "A businessman can't acquire too much broadening," says Delaware & Hudson's William White. "If a person ever stops learning, he's going to die on the vine."

It was precisely in this belief that, ten years ago, Container Corp.'s chairman Walter Paepcke established an intellectual spa at Aspen, Colorado, dedicated to the proposition that "the nose to the grindstone is a useful, necessary and becoming posture for business, but there is more to the world than can easily be seen from this position." Since the founding of Paepcke's Aspen Institute for Humanistic Studies, no fewer than four hundred executives have attended seminars there, discussing everything from Aristotle, Plato and Thucydides, to the writings of Henry Agard Wallace and Robert A. Taft. Every year at Aspen there are about ten two-week seminars, to which men from all walks of life are invited, and it is not unusual for such traditional antagonists as Walter Reuther and a top management negotiator to find themselves across the table from one another, trying to relate the Melian Dialogues to twentieth-century affairs.

Among the top men who have attended the Aspen meetings are chairman C. J. McCarthy of Chance Vought Aircraft, Motorola's Robert Galvin, Hart Schaffner & Marx's

Meyer Kestnbaum, and president David Hill of Pittsburgh Plate Glass, who went to Aspen not under company auspices, but on his own. They come away spouting praise for the program. "Aspen represents not only a unique but an outstandingly worthwhile project for the betterment of America in the broadest sense," says Montgomery Ward's chairman John A. Barr. Inland Steel's Clarence Randall, who was among the early participants, says: "I am still in a very warm glow over my adventure at Aspen. It has done a great deal for me. The discipline involved in facing up to that many keen minds, both to say what you believe and to think out why you believe it, is a very salutary experience. It ought to be required for every man holding substantial responsibility in the business world."

One thing Aspen does for the top executives who go there, which they usually cannot do for themselves, is to give them a change of atmosphere as well as a change of scene. Sure enough, for many corporate presidents, the weekend provides a change of scene—but that is about all. They keep right on working. Atlanta retailer Richard Rich says he is not "one of these guys who lives his work." Yet he gets up early on Sunday morning, makes his own breakfast if the cook isn't there (one egg, two cups of tea, bran flakes and skim milk), and if the weather is nice he dons dark glasses and sits at a card table by his tennis court, working in the sun. The Matson line's president Sevier has a country place fifty miles north of San Francisco, where he goes on weekends, and he always takes a brief case with him. "I find it relaxing going through it in the country," he says.

Obviously, this kind of routine does not leave much time for sports or hobbies, and a number of bosses have given up golf because they found it so time consuming. The Bank of America's president Beise, for example, now putters around his San Mateo garden in blue jeans, instead of tramping the fairways. "I have found that one of the most difficult things to grow is grass," he says. Motorola's president Galvin gave up golf and took up water skiing, a sport in which his whole family can join. The Galvins also bought a farm on which to bring up their children. "Our parents weren't outdoor people," he explains, "but we thought we'd like to acquire an interest in hunting and fishing, and develop an interest in nature to pass along as a heritage to our children."

Nevertheless, golf is still the favorite weekend sport for those who can tear themselves away. Socony Mobil's Albert Nickerson, who joined a country club for the first time only five years ago, now is a regular golfer. So is Jones & Laughlin's president Avery Adams. Bell & Howell's Percy plays an occasional game, at conventions and the like, with I.B.M.'s Tom Watson and president Keith Funston of the New York Stock Exchange. "We try to get somebody in our foursome who shoots 100 or more," he says. Two of the better men on the links are Philip Morris's president Joseph Cullman, who can boast a handicap of five, and General Dynamics' chairman Frank Pace, who also shoots in the seventies.

A championship-level player on the squash racquets and paddle tennis courts alike, Pace heads the list of the more active executive sportsmen. But there are others. Donald Douglas, Jr., likes to spend an occasional day chasing mountain lions in the West. On winter weekends, Tom Watson bundles his wife and children off to his house at Stowe, Vermont, for some skiing. Pickle maker Jack Heinz is equally at home on skis, or clad in mask and flippers for spear fishing. Merck's president Connor, a former baseball, basketball and hockey player, says somewhat apologetically: "I'm now active only in ice skating, golf, swimming, tennis and sailing."

Among the spectator sportsmen, few are more dedicated than General Telephone & Electronics' beefy chairman Donald Power, who has missed very few Ohio State football games since he graduated in 1922. A former trustee of the university, Power commutes from New York to Columbus by plane on fall weekends to root the Buckeyes home.

For the No. 1 men, the most popular indoor sports probably are bridge and poker, which they play to win even though the stakes may not endanger their financial solvency. One of the coolest poker players around is American Airlines' C. R. Smith. "If he were playing for nothing, the game would still be as merciless," says one of Smith's regular poker-playing cronies.

By and large, they are not heavy drinkers, usually taking a drink at lunch only out of courtesy to their guests. (Freeport Sulphur's courtly Langbourne Williams invariably says to any luncheon guest in his office dining room: "Will you break your rule, sir, and have a martini before lunch today?") But there are a very few glaring exceptions. One top industrialist makes for the bar, and stays there, at almost every function he attends. He has been known, after too many martinis, scotches and brandies, to commit some egregious social blunders, such as falling asleep at the dinner table, but he has never been known to let his work suffer the next morning.

Despite the demands on their time, there are some dedicated hobbyists among the top executives. W. R. Grace &

Co.'s Peter Grace, a onetime six-goal polo player, lists his hobbies, somewhat somberly, as "economics and anti-Communism." Harllee Branch likes to sketch pictures of buildings. Bill Paley, Jack Heinz and railroader Pat McGinnis all are art collectors. Roger Blough likes to wander through antique shops. Crawford Greenewalt, who used to play the clarinet in his spare time, now devotes himself, as noted earlier, to recording the life and times of the hummingbird with his camera. With the help of some friends from M.I.T., he has worked out an electronic contraption that triggers the shutter when a hummingbird comes to feed, and Greenewalt's camera stops the bird dead in flight. Chairman Edgar Queeny of Monsanto Chemical, who like Greenewalt is a trustee of New York's American Museum of Natural History, is a recognized naturalist. He has been on expeditions all over the world, and his movies of Alaskan bears and underwater films of salmon spawning are among the most remarkable nature pictures ever taken.

Predictably enough, one of the most avid hobbyists is Atlanta's banker Mills Lane. To begin with, he is an antique car aficionado, numbering among his proud possessions (in addition to his spanking new Rolls Royce) two old Packards, a Ford, a Lincoln and an ancient London taxi that he bought for £40. "Your hobbies have a way of producing results," Lane says. "There ain't no telling how much business I've gotten from my antique cars." He first got interested in old cars when he spotted an ancient Rolls owned by mail-order man Fred Spiegel (Lane's Citizens & Southern bank now does business with Spiegel, Inc.). Lane ran across another prospective customer when the president of a brass company wrote him for advice on how to recondition an ancient car he was working on. Does Lane now do business with the brass company? "Yessuh!" he explodes.

Lane's desk drawers are a clutter of junk, including a pistol made by Eli Whitney—"the first bit of machinery with interchangeable parts ever mass produced in this country"—and framed pictures of antique cars in various states of repair. A corner closet in his office is piled high with necktie boxes, containing bright-colored cravats of Lane's own design—a bale of cotton at top and bottom, a beaming sun and the Lane motto, "It's a wonderful world," in the middle. (Lane has given away more than six hundred of the ties to startled visitors in the past few years.) In another closet is a brace of ancient violins, silent tribute to Lane's status as unofficial violin appraiser for the State of Georgia—a title won when word got in the papers that a friend had shown Lane an old fiddle, which turned out to be a Stradivarius. "Before I knew it," Lane says, "folks were writing me from all over the state, saying they had violins they thought were Stradivariuses, so I told 'em to send 'em in and we'd have 'em appraised."

Aside from the violins, antique cars, neckties and Eli Whitney relics, Lane has another consuming passion: Hawaiian music, which he likes to listen to and to play on his guitar. Whenever a troupe of touring Hawaiian musicians hits Atlanta, Lane asks them out to his house for a Hawaiian hoedown. "I know 'em all," he says proudly. "I guess I have the best collection of Hawaiian music in Atlanta!" There are those who suspect that any day now Lane will be opening a branch of his bank in the nation's fiftieth state.

For years, it was fashionable for the top executives to take few if any vacations, and some of them still follow the practice of just sneaking a few days off here and there during the course of a year. "I haven't had a day's vacation in two years," reports seventy-six-year-old Sam Goldwyn. "It's the spirit of 76." (Goldwyn is able to forget about his business when playing croquet, a sport that keeps him occupied for five or six hours every Saturday and Sunday.) "I haven't had a real holiday since 1941," says Robert P. Koenig, president of Cerro de Pasco (copper mining). And Patrick McGinnis of the Boston & Maine flatly states: "I take no vacations."

But most of the top men these days make a point of getting away for anywhere from three weeks to two months every year (Royal Little of Textron manages to take three months in the summer, and ten days each Christmas and Easter when his school-age son is on vacation). President Lawrence Appley of the American Management Association supplies an interesting explanation for this more relaxed approach to vacation taking.

"For years," he says, "our business executives got bombarded for their Cadillacs, their chauffeurs, their beautiful homes, their golf; they were caricatured and ridiculed, and they crawled into their shells and gave up the high life. They took this thing very hard, while at the same time the size and complexity of their jobs were increasing. For a while it was smart not to take a vacation, to stay in the office from 7 A.M. to 10 P.M. or midnight; this was a complex they developed. But out of this has been coming the professional manager, and now the man is ordered to get out of the office—he must take a month off, and if he can't he mustn't be running and organizing his life and work right. Some reason is coming back into the picture. Executives are learning to staff themselves properly. They are learning that they no longer have to be the best player on the ball club and handle the biggest accounts themselves."

G.E.'s chairman Cordiner, who takes four weeks' vacation a year, insists that his executives take ample time off, too. "I tell a man, 'If you can't take a vacation, there must be something wrong with your department.'"

What do they do when school lets out? A great many of them head straight for the trout stream or the hunting lodge. Owens-Illinois's J. P. Levis, for example, who has been on several African safaris, maintains a hunting and fishing lodge within fifty miles of his Toledo home, which he uses as an occasional hideout (and also as a place to entertain for business). Stanley Allyn of National Cash Register can hardly wait for the grouse season to open in Scotland each year. And Meyer Kestnbaum talks fondly of fishing as "about the only thing I do that calls for real quiet." It may be that fishing and hunting are so popular among the men at the top because these sports afford a measure of quiet and solitude that is rare in their workaday lives.

On their vacation travels, some of the top executives make a big family affair of it. In the summer of 1958 Tom Watson, for example, bought a sailing yacht in Germany and spent the better part of two months cruising the Baltic with his wife and five of his six children (the baby didn't go along). But even when traveling, many find it impossible to escape work. "There are damn few places you can go where you get away from the retailing business," says Dallas' Stanley Marcus. "Either you see customers, or you see things the customers should be wearing. You go to Florida, and you learn that they're wearing this or that in Florida this year, or in Cuba you find someone manufacturing straw bags and you think maybe you should sell them. I guess basically you don't want to forget about your business. The most exciting times I have are on trips to Europe in pursuit of merchandise."

To make up for the time they must spend away from home, some of the men at the top take their wives along on business trips. The women may enjoy the occasional trip to New Orleans, New York or abroad, but their days can be just as lonely in far-off places as at home—and sometimes the far-off places are not quite what the ladies expect them to be. Mrs. Edgar Kaiser, for instance, often accompanies her husband on his many expeditions, but Kaiser confesses that "sometimes she would rather see something other than a plant site or an iron ore mine in her travels."

It doesn't take a marriage counselor to figure out that the executive life calls for a good deal of understanding on the part of the executive wife. Not only does she have to put up with her husband's relentless drive, but often she must nurture it by acting as a sort of buffer for her No. 1 man. "She has to protect you," says Ralph Cordiner, who thanks his wife for protecting him from too much socializing on weekends, among other things.

Almost to a man, the bosses regret that they haven't more time to spend with their families. Cordiner is one of them, but he thinks enforced absence can sometimes be a blessing in disguise. He says that because he had to be away so much his four daughters became self-reliant at a tender age. "You might say we practiced decentralization on them early," he says.

Is it possible for the top executives to spend more time at home? A few seem to manage, by careful planning. "I insist on doing so, and I organize my work accordingly," says Merck's President Connor. "When I get committed to two or at the most three evening dates per week, I refuse all others." General Telephone & Electronics' Donald Power half jokingly suggests that the question is not whether he can find time for his family, but whether they can find time for *him*, so busy are their social lives. "Providing time for family life," he says, "is the responsibility of each member of the family. We all can plan for this as we plan our time for all our activities."

But most of the men at the top think it's easier said than done. Merritt-Chapman & Scott's Louis Wolfson, whose big-dealing might be expected to keep him deskbound, does his best to make more time for his family. But like many others he gets indifferent results.

Wolfson may spend five weeks at his New York office and the next two at home in Miami Beach. When in New York, he spends "the usual nine to five at my desk. Unless a dinner engagement requires otherwise, I usually put in another five to seven hours of work in my hotel suite." When in Miami, he works in an office in his house. "I never take business beyond its door," he says. "I leave it for meals with the family and for after-dinner romps with our youngsters. When they've gone off to bed, I usually get back to work—in my office. I need the comparatively few hours I can spend with the family, and will not permit business to interfere with them."

If a man is to devote himself to his work, Wolfson says, "a great part of the time and effort that normally would be expended on one's children must be given instead to the demands of business. The result often is that a man's wife must shoulder a disproportionate share of the responsibilities for raising the children."

Wolfson speaks for an army of others when he says: "As one who enjoys nothing more than being a family man, this situation undoubtedly has been the greatest sacrifice I've had to make."

But it is a sacrifice that most of the men at the top accept.

# 10.

# THE

# CIVIC LIFE

IT IS NOT JUST THE PRESSURE of business alone, of course, that keeps the top businessmen so busy. From the moment they step on the managerial escalator—and often before—the demands of outside activities begin to rise. The telephone rings—"Say, Harry, we need some help in raising money for that new ambulance unit"; or, "Bill, how'd you like to lend a hand in starting up our new scout troop?" And the letters pour in: "Dear George: As you know, our 25th anniversary blow-out is only two years off, and the Class Committee has selected you . . ."

From schools and colleges, from Red Cross and Red Feather, from libraries, museums and the Y, and from civic and charitable organizations whose existence was almost unknown until this morning's mail, the requests for time and money pile up. There are lunches and dinners to attend and support, late-afternoon meetings, gatherings even on Saturdays and Sundays. "My chief hate in life is the grand ballroom of the Waldorf," grumbles a New York tobacco man whose second hate in life is the Waldorf's chicken-à-la-charity-dinner. "Every damn week, it seems, some new thing comes up," says C.B.S.'s Bill Paley, who now finds himself on the boards of institutions ranging from a Long Island hospital to the Museum of Modern Art. Tom Watson, who is a trustee of Brown University, New York's Memorial Hospital, and the American Museum of Natural History, among others, has been trying to cut down on his extracurricular activities, to devote more time to his family, but he says: "It takes a certain amount of experience to say no."

When Jack Connor first became president of Merck in 1955, he soon found himself becoming entangled in a web of civic jobs. Finally, he decided to concentrate his efforts on one at a time, and to rotate the jobs from year to year, to do the most good and be the most effective. "I've come to the conclusion," Connor says, "that the hundreds of dinner meetings you're invited to, with very few exceptions, don't amount to a damn. The speeches are routine, and the contacts you're supposed to make are much overrated."

Be that as it may, the road of do-goodism has served as a golden highway for more than one man on his way to the top. At a Boy Scout or Community Chest meeting, the up-an-coming executive suddenly may find himself hobnobbing with, and first-naming, the business leaders of his town. He is invited to dinner; he joins a club; he is on his way.

Because of this natural progression, the suspicion rises that perhaps the businessmen who become most active in community affairs do so primarily for business reasons—and indeed it is difficult to draw an absolute definition of motives. Most men get involved in charitable and civic affairs for what they honestly believe are altruistic reasons, and no doubt the measure of altruism is large. Railroader

Wayne Johnston, for example, says: "Having been raised a poor boy, I believe one should give back to society, both in money and time, commensurate with one's success." Johnston "gives back to society" by working for the Boy Scouts, the Y.M.C.A., Chicago's Old Peoples Home (of which he is president), and two universities, to name a few of his extracurricular activities.

Many of the public-spirited executives plainly enjoy their extracurricular activity, finding in it the kind of reward and breadth of experience that does not always come their way in the normal course of business. Retailer Stanley Marcus, for example, clearly gets a kick out of his work as an overseer of Harvard College, and is fascinated by some of the things he has learned in that capacity.

There is, too, a rewarding sense of humanity that goes with much community work—and the pleasure of getting things done with others. As one executive put it not so elegantly, "It's nice to find out that the other fellow isn't always a stinker."

Nevertheless, there is no question that good community work also is good public relations—both for the executive and for his company—and it is not surprising to find that many of those who work the hardest in the public interest are in businesses such as banking, insurance, utilities and retailing, which deal most directly with the public. Atlanta's J. J. McDonough, president of Georgia Power, has run the statewide Easter Seal campaign, and has been president of both the state and local chambers of commerce. "You can't separate personal interest from corporate interest," he once said. "Everybody is our customer and public service is bound to relate back to business. But that isn't the purpose."

The time that the top men spend on outside activities ranges from a few hours a month to nine full months a year —as in the case of Ivan Allen, Jr., vice chairman of Atlanta's Ivan Allen Co., the largest office-supply company in the Southeast. Allen once estimated that 80 per cent of his time was taken up with civic activities. "I've made some money," he said, "I've inherited some money. I've had a good business to work with. Let's put it this way: The 'rent' we pay for being here and having this opportunity is somehow discharged in the civic contributions we make." Chairman John Greene of Ohio Bell Telephone figures that in one year, when he was a top man in the local Community Fund and also president of the Cleveland Welfare Federation, he attended no fewer than 280 meetings. President Howard J. Morgens of Procter & Gamble, who is a director or trustee of eight organizations, ranging from the American Heritage Foundation to the Children's Home in Cincinnati, figures he spends about 20 per cent of his working hours on such affairs.

All around the country, most of the civic, charitable and cultural organizations are pretty much run by top businessmen—and different money-raising drives often are run by the same people. "I've noticed that in any city you go to, it's always the same group of people who get into charity drives, civic work and the like," says Cleveland's Dwight Joyce, who himself is mixed up in half a score of civic projects. Why don't the others enter in? Is it because they are too busy? "It's because they're just plain selfish," Joyce says.

This means that the unselfish have to take on a tremendous load. New York's hard-working J. Peter Grace, for example, lists no fewer than twenty civic and charitable endeavors that he is "principally" interested in, ranging from the Catholic Youth Organization, of which he is president, to Boys Clubs of America, of which he is a director. Philip Pillsbury, of the milling company, numbers the following jobs among his outside interests: vice chairman, Yale Alumni Board; trustee (and past president), Minnesota Orchestral Association; and director, Family & Children's Service, Minneapolis.

The part-time jobs make up a varied array. Henry Alexander of the Morgan Guaranty, for example, is vice president of the Board of Trust of Vanderbilt University, his alma mater; vice president and trustee of New York City's Presbyterian Hospital; treasurer of the Downtown Lower Manhattan Association, and a trustee of the Metropolitan Museum of Art. National Cash Register's Stanley Allyn has been president of the United Community Funds and Councils of America, and campaign chairman for the American National Red Cross. In Buffalo, National Gypsum's chairman Melvin Baker, who estimates that he spends 10 per cent of his time on such activities, has concerned himself with matters ranging from cancer (for three years chairman of the American Cancer Crusade for New York State) to the Bible (chairman of National Bible Week in 1956), and lately has spent a good deal of time on matters of urban renewal and redevelopment. J. P. Levis of Owens-Illinois, who lists more than a dozen extracurricular activities, recently finished raising $2 million for a new engineering-science college for the University of Toledo.

One of the busiest and most effective do-gooders is Burroughs Corp.'s president Ray R. Eppert, recently head of the United Foundation of Metropolitan Detroit and vice president of the United Community Funds & Councils of America. In this capacity alone, Eppert delivered nine speeches in as many states in 1957, seventeen speeches in thirteen states in 1956, and sixteen speeches in 1955. His many interests range from the Boy Scouts and boys clubs to mental health and polio, and Eppert once estimated (to *Newsweek's* Detroit Bureau Chief James Jones) that he spends 15 per cent of his week and 25 per cent of his weekends working on civic affairs.

During one 1958 week, he had these affairs, outside of his Burroughs work, to attend to:

Monday: An Eagle Scout dinner meeting.

Tuesday: Made a luncheon speech to the Harper Hospital Auxiliary, talking about a trip he had made to Russia.

Friday: Attended a lunchtime executive board meeting of the Detroit-Tomorrow Committee.

(Eppert spent Wednesday in Philadelphia on business, flew to Washington that night and spent Thursday with Army brass from the Pentagon, discussing Army accounting problems as related to electronic computers.)

Eppert is invited to join about three additional organizations each week, ranging from business to educational and community groups. How does he pick and choose? "You try to evaluate [a request] from the standpoint of whether it is important. . . . If so, do you feel that you can contribute something? If so, can you actually participate? Are you able to give a hand, and not just a name? I have very little patience with the person who will just join up, and not do anything, or be able to do anything."

Among the thousands of top men who devote their time and effort to hundreds of charitable, educational and civic groups, it would be impossible to pick the do-bester. But if a tournament of do-gooders were held, one of the finalists most certainly would be C. Allen Harlan of Detroit. President of Harlan Electric Co., and president, director or part owner of fifteen affiliated companies throughout the Midwest and East, Harlan's business interests alone—to say nothing of his wife, Ivabell, and seven children—would seem to be numerous enough to demand his attention seven days and seven nights a week.

But Harlan in 1958 still found time to be an active member of more than a score of extracurricular organizations.*

One entire wall and parts of the other three walls of Harlan's Detroit office are covered with citations, awards, certificates, commissions, photographs and other memorabilia of his civic service.

Why does Harlan spend so much time on extracurricular activities? "All these companies around here," he once told a visitor, waving an arm to indicate a big chunk of Detroit industry, "they spend thousands and millions of dollars on public relations. I'm my own public relations," he added with disarming candor. Harlan is quite genuinely con-

---

* At fifty, he held the following posts: president, Educational TV Foundation (Detroit); trustee, Bethany College; trustee, Fisk University; trustee, Hampton Institute; member, State Board of Agriculture (Michigan State University); fellow, Brandeis University (to which he claims to be "the first non-Jew to give scholarship money"); board member, Boy Scouts of America; board member, Y.M.C.A.; board member, International Institute; board member, Community Health Association; trustee, Burton Mercy Hospital; advisory member, Michigan Economic Development Commission; vice president, director, United Foundation; advisory board member, American Red Cross; member of board and finance committee, Junior Achievement; board member, American Association for the United Nations; board member, Michigan Society for Mental Health (Wayne County Chapter); board member, Detroit Urban League; board member, United Service Organization; board member, Detroit Council of Churches; member, Labor Participation Committee, United Health & Welfare Fund of Michigan; board member, Metropolitan Detroit Building Fund; trustee, National Jewish Hospital at Denver.

cerned with the betterment of mankind. But to a *Newsweek* reporter he conceded frankly: "I'm the trouble shooter and I'm the guy who brings in business [for my companies]. The tools that I use to bring in business are all these activities. They open a lot of doors. Everything you do in life must be commercially feasible."

Harlan mentioned the president of a large Midwestern university which has benefited grandly through Harlan's scholarship program. "Whenever he talks to a contractor who is bidding on a new construction project at the university," Harlan says, "he tells the contractor that the electrical work will be done by C. Allen Harlan." But if this seems unduly commercial, it should be noted that at the same time many a student has graduated from that university who would not have managed to do so without Harlan's financial aid. "Unless I make money, I won't have much to give, will I?" Harlan asks matter-of-factly.

Walter Laidlaw, executive vice president of the United Foundation in Detroit, said of him: "Mr. Harlan is the great extrovert. He gets up before a meeting and preaches. [In one fund-raising drive] he took a hillbilly band out to the construction jobs, and he was most effective in preaching to workers on the job as a Tennessee preacher might." In the year Harlan first was made head of the Building Industry Committee of the United Foundation in Detroit, he had a target to shoot at—the previous year, $40,000 had been raised. "In our first year," he reported later, "we brought in $140,000. In the second year it was $280,000, and in the third, $360,000."

Harlan started giving money for scholarships after his discharge from the Navy in 1945 (he was a lieutenant). "My wife and I wanted the scholarships to cross all color and creed lines," he said. Their first gift was to the University of Tennessee, and in the five years to 1958 Harlan's and his company's scholarship donations amounted to more than $100,000 annually. He has established scholarships at, among others, the University of Michigan, Michigan State, Wayne State, Brandeis, Bethany, Fisk, Berea College, Union College, and Hampton Institute.

Civic work is such a time-consuming affair that it is a wonder corporations let their executives get mixed up in it at all. But they do; in fact they encourage it. As in the case of the executives themselves, again it is difficult to delineate the corporate motives, since by the nature of the work there has to be a mixture of altruism and self-interest. But the fact that the public interest is a motivation at all marks a notable change in the corporate approach to the world.

In his book, *The Twentieth Century Capitalist Revolution*, Adolf Berle, Jr., made the point with some eloquence: ". . . the fact seems to be that the really great corporation managements have reached a position for the first time in their history in which they must consciously take account of philosophical considerations. They must consider the kind of a community in which they have faith, and which they will serve, and which they intend to help construct and maintain. . . ." While some businessmen, as Berle correctly noted, are suspicious of community planning, "the greatest leaders in the corporate field take a contrary view. They forcefully argue that corporations are always citizens of the community in which they operate, while large ones necessarily play a mighty part in the life of their time. It is not possible for them, these men state, to carry on great corporate businesses apart from the main context of American life. If private business and businessmen do not assume community responsibilities, government must step in and American life will become increasingly statist."

Thus it is that such men as Jones & Laughlin's Avery Adams and United Aircraft's H. M. Horner talk about the corporation's responsibility to be a "good corporate citizen." And thus it is that in some communities companies actually pool their junior executives and lend them to major money-raising drives for weeks at a time. Corporations have become so civic-minded, in fact, that a few top executives are beginning to think they have gone too far. "Up until now," says J. P. Levis, "I have believed that the role of industry in these matters should be an ever-increasing one. Now I am beginning to wonder how far it should go. [Is it possible] that an over-participation on the part of corporations in certain charitable activities is . . . reducing the public responsibility of the individual? Charitable institutions are more and more depending on corporate contributions and less and less on the generosity of the individual. While I believe that a corporation is a good deal more than just a profit machine, I am beginning to have some doubts as to the extent of the role the corporation should play in community, charitable and educational activities."

Good conscience and good public relations are not the only corporate motivations for encouraging executives to do good. Many companies also look on community work as a fine way to develop men—and to build a sense of individuality by making decentralization even more meaningful. In Chicago, for example, Motorola has long been jogging its plant managers around the country to get active as individuals in their communities. Motorola is proud of the fact that two of them have been presidents of their local chambers of commerce, and one has been a mayor.

When there is a hospital to be built in a Motorola community, president Robert Galvin tells his local plant manager: "Don't ask us; *tell* us how much you think we should give." One Motorola vice president, in Phoenix, was instrumental in establishing a new engineering school there, working closely with the president of the University of Arizona. "He reported in from time to time," says Galvin, "and finally he had to put his money where his mouth was." Motorola agreed to kick in $50,000 a year for three years.

How good a job do the businessmen do-gooders do? Robert Moses, who as New York City's Commissioner of Parks and a guiding spirit of the Lincoln Center for the Performing Arts has long been in a position to judge, is one who is generally encouraged by their approach. Moses wrote recently: "The partnership of self-appointed patrons of the arts with elected officialdom is relatively new in this country and needs a lot of cultivating. In its worst manifestations we find the eccentricities of wealth uncomfortably bracketed with the vagaries of politics, the troglodyte tycoon with assorted prejudices, uneasy in the salon and theatre, sitting beside the hard-boiled, uncouth politician who wants his brother-in-law to play the traps, or his lady friend to sing Mimi. At best, it brings together for the common good the occasional cultivated bureaucrat with the truly dedicated citizen, the economic royalist, and the business Bourbon. In any event it makes for a new, fascinating and fruitful companionship in the music of the spheres and hastens that biblical day when the morning

156

stars will sing together and all the sons of God will shout for joy."

In dabbling with more terrestrial music, it seems that the rule is for the public-spirited businessmen to exercise a marked degree of restraint. A top man in the music business who has observed the situation at first hand for years has this to say: "Most businessmen who get interested in symphony orchestras do it as a hobby, because they like music. They don't necessarily know anything about it, and usually, to their credit, they will infuse the management of an orchestra with money and business brains, then hire a musical director and leave it pretty much up to him to run the show." A case in point is New York's David Keiser, chairman of the Cuban-American Sugar Co., and a concert-stature musician himself, who is now president of the New York Philharmonic. As much as anyone, he was responsible for hiring Leonard Bernstein, and for the rebirth of a famous orchestra that had fallen on bad times.

While businessmen can be effective in the realm of the arts, not every civic project they undertake ends up as a tribute to pure aesthetics and good taste. Probably no businessmen have done more for their city than have the leaders of Pittsburgh industry, who have co-operated to literally rebuild their town and convert its atmosphere from grime to glitter. Yet there is a certain soulless quality to the metal-clad buildings of Pittsburgh's new Gateway Center. Lawyer Leland Hazard peered out his office window at the gleaming new structures one day not long ago, and commented sadly: "There is an insensitivity. It's not venal or malicious. These buildings are in nondescript taste. They represent a disbelief in professionalism. Do you realize they were started without an architect?"

Hazard paced around his office and continued: "The disrespect for professionalism is a concomitant of mass production. The production engineer deals with very few people; his life is devoted to getting a penny a pound off the cost of his product. He is subject to few influences. Merchants by necessity deal with many more people; the act of trade is cosmopolitan, disparate, random; the merchant must go to the centers of style. But the big industrialists have no time, no necessity, for such exposure." Hazard took another lap around the office. "A few of us think about this," he said. "I suspect that Pittsburgh is the last vestige of Puritanism—a cultural pocket has developed here. To switch the metaphor, a few funerals would break the log jam. This town is Florence without Lorenzo; it is ready for cultural leadership."

Whether cultural leadership will come to Pittsburgh, only time will tell. But it is a sure thing that if money can buy it—as it can buy homes for orphans or scholarships for needy students—the businessmen of Pittsburgh will find the cash, as businessmen all over the U.S. have been successfully doing. A spokesman for one Los Angeles charity says: "The average person in professional fund raising isn't too imaginative or professional. When you get a top businessman in to show you how to run a campaign, you get a less costly campaign and one that brings in money. Businessmen know each other and they know where the money is, and they don't have to go hat in hand or apologizing, as the regular fund raiser is apt to do."

And if the businessmen themselves happen to benefit incidentally from their own good works, what matter? Wasn't there a parable about casting bread upon the waters?

# 11.

## CLUB MEN ALL

IT IS TEN MINUTES before noon in Pittsburgh, on almost any weekday of the year, and there is a pre-luncheon spurt of activity in executive offices all over town. In modernistic surroundings high in the Alcoa Building, president Frank Magee of the Aluminum Co. of America finishes his morning chores, claps on his hat and makes for the door. A couple of blocks away, at 525 William Penn Place, Big Steel's president Walter F. Munford makes a final phone call, signs a letter and is on his way. At about the same instant, the morning's affairs are being wound up by the top executives at Gulf, at Koppers, at the Mellon Bank, at Pittsburgh Coke & Chemical.

What makes this familiar routine noteworthy in Pittsburgh is that every one of these men at the top is hurrying off to have lunch at exactly the same place, just as he does day in, day out, winter, spring, summer and fall. The executive gathering place is a brownstone pile named the Duquesne Club, and within its solid walls at noon each day can be found a greater aggregation of managerial talent than in any other eating place in the country, and perhaps the world. The Duquesne is the *ne plus ultra* of business clubs in the United States.

The green-awninged clubhouse on Pittsburgh's Sixth

**159**

Avenue has a long tradition of gentility and wealth that infects the club's entire staff, from head telephone operator Bessie, who has been there fifty-five years, and Chef Abel Bomberault (formerly of the old Ritz in New York), who with his chief helpers has been there close to thirty years, down to the newest bellhop. Cynics may argue that good pay and lavish tips have something to do with the infection; a Duquesne doorman, it is said, can clear as much as $15,-000 a year, including the tips that he collects at Christmastime, when chauffeur-driven company limousines drive up to dispense discreet envelopes to the staff. But one porter with a mere eight years of Duquesne Club service puts it this way: "This place grows on you. You just can't leave. It's the kind of people, and the atmosphere."

The kind of people who belong to the Duquesne—and who have always belonged—are the leading men of Pittsburgh industry. The club's 1958-59 president, for example, is Clifford Hood, recently retired president of U.S. Steel. (Hood succeeded Alcoa's Magee as president of the Duquesne, and Magee in turn succeeded Jones & Laughlin's Avery Adams.) The club's first vice president is William K. Whiteford, president of Gulf Oil; its second vice president is Edward J. Hanley, president of Allegheny Ludlum. On its membership rolls can be found the top men from every Pittsburgh line of endeavor, from banking to pickle making—including two Mellons, three Heinzes, five Follansbees and six Hillmans. For years, when John L. Lewis talked of the coal operators he used to refer to his adversaries as "the boys at the Duquesne Club." As someone else once said, the Duquesne can claim "the least underprivileged membership in town."

The kind of atmosphere that belongs to the Duquesne

is as old-fashioned as the club building's oaken paneling and columns; as quiet as the portrait of bearded Andrew Carnegie (presented by Mrs. Carnegie) that stares down from one wall; as well-ordered and deliberate as the huge grandfather clock that marks off the hours and the years in the first-floor reading room.

Founded in 1873 and at its present location since 1889, the Duquesne represents the fulfillment, American style, of man's age-old urge to gather with congenial male companions of similar background and interests. This instinct, together with, perhaps, the loneliness that goes with a command position, has made a club man out of almost every top-rank American executive, and there are but few who cannot claim at least one city club and one country club in their *Who's Who* listings.

Among the earliest clubs on record were the religious societies of ancient Greece and Rome, which tended to become political organizations as time passed. Often, they were opposed to the state; one Grecian club required each and every member to pledge: "I will be an enemy to the people, and will devise all the harm I can against them."

American clubs are in quite a different tradition, of course. The modern-day version of club life and sociability began to emerge in the coffeehouses of seventeenth-century London, where men would gather to discuss the arts and sciences and political issues of the day. In twentieth-century America, conversations in the clubs may not sparkle with the wit and learning of a Samuel Johnson. The talk may be mostly business, but the purpose of the club is the same: to provide a congenial meeting place for men of mutual interests.

Many American clubs outrank the Duquesne on one

count or another. Pittsburgh's own Rolling Rock country club, fifty miles out of town, numbers many Duquesners among its members—but only the *crème de la crème*. "They don't get the sales managers there," says one Duquesne oldtimer. To cite another example, New York's Links Club is smaller than the Duquesne, but for its size probably can boast a greater density of big names, including George Humphrey, Winthrop Aldrich, Lucius Clay, Henry Ford II, Neil McElroy, Frank Pace—and Dwight D. Eisenhower. Not long ago, a lunch was held there for New York's Governor Rockefeller, a Links member himself. As some of the guests came down in the elevator after lunch, one of them remarked enthusiastically, "Well, I think we've just had lunch with the next President of the United States." A uniformed Links employee answered, with more than a trace of hauteur: "We have served lunch to a lot of *them*, sir."

A number of clubs are older than the Duquesne, or bigger, or more exclusive. In Detroit, for instance, the Yondetega Club is so select that more than one newsman has had trouble even finding out where it is. And a number are stuffier. The stronghold of Chicago's business leaders is the Chicago Club, where some stomachs rumble at the thought of "Modern Republicanism" and begin to ache severely at the merest mention of Walter Reuther. In this institution, there are two clubs-within-a-club, which have regular luncheon meetings—Room 100, a group of fifty men including an Armour, a Swift, Sewell Avery, and Marshall Field, Jr.; and Room 803 which numbers among its members another Swift, former Yale football star Clint Frank (who is now a top Chicago advertising man), publisher John S. Knight, and Walter Paepcke.

But for sheer weight of numbers and depth of resources, the Duquesne has all the others beat. "There's nothing in Chicago or Philadelphia that comes anywhere near the Duquesne," boasts secretary and treasurer Gurdon Flagg, who with his family lives in the club and has guided its affairs for more than a quarter of a century. "There are a couple in New York that come pretty close—the Union Club and the Union League are both nice. But no club has the facilities that we do, or gets the play at lunch. We serve lunch to 1,000 people every day, and they're all top notch. The Duquesne Club has always had the distinction of being able to draw the top people."

The Duquesne is in marked contrast to many U.S. clubs on another score, as well. In recent years a number of them have been fighting off the intrusion of business affairs into what are supposed to be purely social gathering places. College clubs, which offer new graduates a sort of beginner's course in club life in America, were the first to be so besieged, and, much to the dismay of the house committees, it is not unusual at all to see contracts, balance sheets and other documents spread out in the public rooms of such places as the Harvard and Yale Clubs of New York. But recently the pressures of business have been mounting within the more strictly social clubs, as well.

A year or two ago, members of San Francisco's sedate Pacific Union Club (known affectionately as the P.U.) received notices advising them that brief cases should not be opened, nor business papers displayed, within the confines of the old club building atop Nob Hill. ("Deplorable that such a notice should have to go out at all," grumbled one shocked P.U. regular. "Next thing you know they'll be telling us not to throw up in the reading room!") At about the same time, members of some of New York's better clubs were wincing at this not-altogether-accurate line in a *Fortune* article on the executive lunch: "At the Metropolitan or the Union League or the University . . . you might do a $10,000 deal, but you'd use the Knickerbocker or the Union or the Racquet for $100,000, and then for $1 million, you'd have to move on to the Brook or the Links."

Where Pittsburgh's Duquesne Club differs is in the fact that it is quite frankly a business club, and always has been. "On its membership rolls," boasts its own Year Book, "somewhere along the way, may be found the names of most of the pioneers and leaders of the iron and steel industry and within its walls have been held many conferences which marked the development of that great industry." One long-time member says: "The way to tell if a fellow's getting along in any Pittsburgh company is to see if he's yet a member of the Duquesne. As soon as his name goes up for membership, you know he ought to be watched. He's a comer."

The club has 1,700 resident members (including more than fifty top-flight employees of U.S. Steel), and 850 nonresidents. It always has a waiting list of about 200, of whom 80 or 90 are admitted each year. The prerequisites for membership are four: $1,000 for the initiation fee, $240 for dues, at least nominal Christianity, and the blessing of your employer, preferably to the extent of his being willing to pay the bills. One man who has been a member of the Duquesne for five years says that he has paid perhaps $30 worth of personal bills himself in that time, while his company has picked up tabs totaling about $6,000. According to no less an authority than secretary-treasurer Gurdon Flagg, "the Duquesne is as near to a business as you can possibly get

As a matter of fact, the club has been fighting a battle for years to prove that it *is* a business. One October day back in 1940, Gurdon Flagg appeared before a Federal judge to argue a tax case for the Duquesne, which was trying to get back $75,000 in taxes paid, on the ground that the club's income from dues should not be taxable since it is a business organization. The U.S. attorney, trying to prove that the Duquesne was a social club, managed to bring out only the fact that on the occasion of one member's eightieth birthday it had allowed candles to be placed on his cake (Flagg hastily explained that the club did not pay for the candles). When the U.S. attorney sought to prove that the Duquesne was the scene of wild parties, particularly on New Year's Eve, Flagg answered that on that particular night of the year, "the place is like a morgue."

In point of fact, that is the normal state of affairs on many nights of the year; it is at lunchtime that the Duquesne comes alive, and it is then that a man can be marked by name, rank, serial number (and salary)—according to where he eats in the club. There are, to begin with, a number of dining rooms, each with its own personality. On the ground floor, there is an oak-paneled, leather-chaired bar, where the second lieutenants of industry are likely to start gathering at noon or a little before (Pittsburghers eat earlier than New Yorkers); by twelve-twenty every table in the bar is taken.

Then, also on the main floor, there is the Patio, an airy, leafy enclosure with wrought-iron furniture, which is reminiscent of the Palm Court in the Plaza Hotel of New York. Here, an insurance man may be seen lunching with a steel company vice president; or there may be the publisher of a trade magazine; or a few retired operating men from the steel and coal industries. At one table a space salesman for a national magazine may be entertaining the advertising manager of a steel company, along with the account executive from the firm's advertising agency. "You never see a president of a steel company in the Patio," says one member.

It is when you go upstairs in the Duquesne that you begin to enter the substratosphere of executive power. On the second floor there are no fewer than five dining rooms, including the main one; and in each of these, day after day, the same people sit at the same tables. As you enter the main dining room, the Gulf Oil table is across the way; Gulf's chairman David Proctor sits facing the door, surrounded by his senior vice presidents. In the corner over to the right is the Koppers table, populated by most of the top men in that company, and next to it is a U.S. Steel table, where sales vice presidents break bread together. In another, smaller room nearby, Pittsburgh Coke & Chemical's president, chairman and vice presidents gather daily; in still another, Pittsburgh Plate Glass has a central spot, while Alcoa's executive committee chairman Roy Hunt holds forth in the corner—next to Jack Heinz's table.

If the Duquesne's second floor feeds the captains of industry, many of the field marshals are to be found on the fourth and fifth floors, where thirty-five suites are rented out by the year (at $12,000 and up) to such companies as U.S. Steel, Gulf Oil, Jones & Laughlin, Blaw-Knox, and Alcoa, to name just a few. These attractively decorated apartments usually have a bedroom, living room and dining room; they are used by the companies' topmost brass for meetings and lunch almost every day, and for dinners perhaps two or three times a week, particularly when a visiting fireman, or rather fire chief, comes to town.

In addition to a bedroom and a bathroom with wall-to-wall carpeting, and a dining room decorated with hand-some early American wallpaper, U.S. Steel's suite has a large living room paneled in light wood, with a television set and a movie screen built into the wall over the fireplace, and hidden from view by sliding paneling when not in use. T. Mellon & Sons' apartment, which like the others is decorated in the grand manner, has hand-painted Chinese wall-paper and not the slightest hint of a "hotelly" look.

In these company suites new products and mergers are planned, bargaining strategy for labor negotiations is hammered out, multimillion-dollar financing arrangements are made. Here, and in the public dining rooms below, the professionals of production get together and exchange ideas, day after day. There is a daily exposure of people to people who are all of the same mold or forced into the same mold. This tends, no doubt, to channel their interests and energies toward the mono-purpose goal of production; and it may well be, as has been said, that Pittsburgh would not be the production marvel it is without the exchange of information, techniques and ideas that takes place every noontime at the Duquesne.

Leland Hazard, who sits at a table with Jones & Laughlin's former boss Admiral Ben Moreell, Westinghouse's chairman Gwilym Price, Alcoa's Frank Magee, and several others, including Austin Pardue, the Episcopal Bishop of Pittsburgh, describes the noontime meal this way: "The conversation is good, even cultivated. Few have read Pasternak, you understand, but they know all about him. There is gossip about business deals in the making, the usual amount of banter, some talk of foreign affairs. They're all Republicans, of course—from the far right [Moreell] to the left [Hazard]. Recently I reminded the table that ten years ago Walter Reuther had suggested that the U.S. contribute ten per cent of the national income to developing the underdeveloped countries. I said that that wasn't one of Reuther's hare-brained schemes. The reaction was silence—respectful, but silence just the same."

It may not be surprising that the members of the Duquesne are Republicans almost to a man, but there *was* a surprise in some political statistics issued by the club a generation ago. In 1936, the Duquesne polled its employees to find out how they were enrolled, and reported that there were 170 Republicans among them, and only 6 Democrats. Democratic Senator Joseph F. Guffey, himself a Duquesne member, promptly charged that the club had used "coercion and intimidation" on its employees to get them to vote for Alf Landon. As it turned out, Guffey need not have worried.

Like many other clubs, the Duquesne shuns publicity. Its doormen will give the fishy eye to anyone suspected of having newspaper connections, and if a member is responsible for the club's name appearing in the papers, an apology is in order. Such was the case back in 1940, when the late Samuel Harden Church, eighty-two, president of the Carnegie Institute and a former Pennsylvania Railroad official, announced to the *New York Times* that he and a group of friends were prepared to pay a reward of $1 million for the capture of Adolf Hitler, and his delivery "alive, unwounded and unhurt" to the League of Nations for trial. Church later denied that many of his accomplices were, as he was quoted as saying in the *Times,* members of the Duquesne. His letter of apology was promptly posted on the bulletin board.

A few years ago, the Duquesne got in the papers not because of anyone duly elected to the club, but because of three armed bandits who elected themselves, pro tem, at the point of a gun. They forced their way into the club, tied up three bewildered employees and made their way for "the little safe," apparently on the reasonable assumption that a little safe in the Duquesne was worth a big one almost anywhere else. The bandits got away with nothing; the trouble was that there is no "little safe" in the club.

Business club though it is, all is not business at the Duquesne. On almost any evening, in one of the many company suites, a table-stakes poker game is under way; and there is a regular Saturday afternoon game of bridge, at two cents a point, for such men as Moreell, Magee, U.S. Steel's ex-boss Ben Fairless and Alcoa's chairman I. W. (Chief) Wilson, who is considered the best player of the lot.

Some years back, the Duquesne was the scene of one of the more elaborate and successful practical jokes ever perpetrated in the upper echelons of U.S. industry. It all began in Detroit, when Chrysler's K. T. Keller invited the late Frank Judson of Pittsburgh Plate Glass to his house for dinner, and cooked the meal himself. When Judson got back to Pittsburgh, he thought it would be funny to have the Duquesne's Gurdon Flagg write Keller offering him a job as chef. But Judson lived to regret the gag.

Keller scribbled out a note of reply on a greasy piece of paper and popped it in the mail to Flagg. It went something like this: "Dear Mr. Flag, Mr. Keller maybe thinks hes a good cooker but i know better. i does the cooking around here and i'd like the job. Signed, Willie Robison." A few days later, going along with the fun, Flagg wrote back saying the job was "Willie's" for the asking. The practical joke was under way.

Keller thereupon hired a professional gagster, who in

turn employed a Negro and sent him off to Pittsburgh with the job offer in his hand. When the phony applicant presented himself to Flagg at the Duquesne Club and demanded the job, Flagg explained that it was all a joke. The applicant remonstrated, and Flagg sent him off to see Judson, who promptly threw him out of his office. Enter the professional practical joker, posing as a lawyer and bearing a warrant for Judson's arrest, supplied by a friendly justice of the peace. "By the time we got through," Keller guffaws, "Frank Judson had paid up $300—which was enough to cover the expenses of the entire joke!"

How does a young man in a hurry get himself elected to the Duquesne?

"We don't let a fellow fill out an application until we know he's all right," says Gurdon Flagg, who himself is "all right" by virtue of being a successful businessman in his own right, running all the restaurants in the Gateway Center and catering to various other organizations around town. (Flagg would rather not talk about his Duquesne salary, "because it's probably more than a lot of the members make themselves.") Once his general "all rightness" has been established, a candidate needs two proposers to vouch for his character, sobriety, background, family, and standing in the business community. Flanked by a proposer, the candidate then goes before the admissions committee, a group of five men who hold regular lunchtime meetings at which they interview aspiring clubmen, one by one. Because the Duquesne, like other clubs, is after young members, a man over forty who meets all the other requirements may have a little more trouble than a younger candidate. Many people have had to wait several years before getting the nod from the membership committee, from Gurdon Flagg—or from their employers.

The various Pittsburgh companies have differing policies regarding the level at which an executive qualifies for having his Duquesne dues and other bills picked up by the corporation. At Alcoa, for example, Flagg would guess that the magic level is the departmental sales manager bracket. On the other hand, some large steel companies will not pay the fare even for so important a man as an advertising director (although there are hopes in Pittsburgh ad circles that this now will change, since one important company recently proposed its advertising director for membership).

Occasionally there will be an opening in the membership ranks for a company that has not one but several executives up for the Duquesne. In a case like this, says Flagg, "the corporation usually lets you know who they want to get in first." Such a case arose not long ago, when there was an opening for one man from a certain steel company which had four of its executives up for membership. A quick telephone conversation between Flagg and the president of the company was all that was needed to determine which of the four men should get the tap. He was duly elected, and suddenly all Pittsburgh—including the three men who did not make the grade—became aware of another young man on his way to the top.

# 12.

# THE DIRECTOR:

# THEORY AND FACT

IN THEORY and in the textbooks, the publicly held American corporation is the epitome of the democratic process. Its owners, the stockholders, elect a board of directors to protect their interests; the board, in turn, selects the company's management (or replaces it if the directors disapprove of the way the company is being run). And if the board fails to protect the stockholders' interests? Why, then the stockholders simply throw the rascals out, electing a new board to take their place.

So goes the theory. But what is the fact? The fact seems to be that in scores and hundreds of corporations the board of directors, supposedly the final power, is not now and never has been an effective force in corporate affairs. Instead of being management's ultimate judge, answerable only to the stockholders, in many companies the board has become an instrument of management. And, too often, the directors have become an oligarchy perpetuating not only themselves but also the management they are supposed to supervise—but which, in fact, probably selected them in the first place.

To cite a not so hypothetical example, what really happens when a board member dies or retires? Chances are the president of the company will draw up a list of possible replacements, perhaps with the help of others on his management team. He will present the likeliest candidate to his board, whose approval often is almost automatic. The board then presents the new name to stockholders at the next annual meeting, and usually their approval is as routine as approving the minutes of the last meeting. The result is that the chief executive often is able to surround himself with directors with whom he has either social or business connections or both, and who as a result are not in a very good position to offer objective criticisms of the man and management that selected them.

In 1956, Columbia University's Graduate School of Business, at the urging of E. Everett Smith, a director for the management consulting firm of McKinsey & Co., held a seminar on the role of the American corporate director. It was attended by a dozen or so topflight managers, including John Connor of Merck, president Charles G. Mortimer of General Foods, M. J. Rathbone of Jersey Standard, and H. J. Heinz II, and at one of the sessions the following colloquy took place:

Participant A: "Now, the thing that really bothers me on this question is this. Since the board is chosen by the chief executive very largely . . . and is submitted to the stockholder for approval (where the approval is always obtained), to what extent is it possible to achieve a completely objective and a critical appraisal of the management program?"

Participant B: "Well, that's what I question. It ought not to be chosen by the chief executive without checks and double checks."

A: "Who should it be chosen by?"

B: "Well, you do it by a committee of the board. They've got to pick their own colleagues."

A: "But do they?"

B: "They don't, I know. . . ."

The notable aspect of this exchange is that the stockholders were considered only as a body that would go through the formalities of approving something already decided by the management or the directors of the company. The fact is that while corporate democracy prevails in theory, in most cases it does not prevail in fact. Except in the rare instance where some minority stockholder or group of stockholders goes to the great effort and expense of waging a proxy fight, what the management and directors say goes. The rule is that if a stockholder these days is dissatisfied with the managers or directors of a company in which he owns stock, he will simply sell his shares and put his money to work elsewhere; he will not choose to fight.

This is not to say that all boards of directors, or even most of them, are bad. But it does point up the fact, too often overlooked, that some of the supposed ground rules of corporate capitalism have somehow been lost in the shuffle. And it raises serious questions about the health of the very core of the capitalistic system.

Why is the board of directors so ineffective in so many companies? Part of the answer is that in many companies management itself has never wanted a strong board. A further answer can be found in the vast changes that have taken place in American business—the trend to bigness and complexity outlined in Chapter 3, and the development of the professional manager noted in Chapter 6. These two related events have had a number of related effects. In the first place, they have combined to turn out a number of chief executives who tend to look at "outsiders" on their boards as a bunch of well-meaning amateurs who cannot possibly get to know enough about the business, on a part-time basis, to make intelligent recommendations.

Then, too, the recent emphasis on professional management and the techniques of getting things done has taken the spotlight off the important role a director can play, from the standpoint of counseling and planning for the future. And because of the glorification of the operating manager, it is not surprising that many chief executives nowadays resent, either consciously or otherwise, the thought that they should be answerable to higher authority. In any case, as management consultant Everett Smith wrote not long ago in the *Harvard Business Review*, "it is ironic that we in this country who have done so much to further the art of management should have so neglected such a vital area as the job of directors."

The blame is shared by managers and directors alike. For their part, too many managers fail to supply their boards with sufficient information and sufficient time in which to study it before a board meeting. Often, a director arriving for the monthly meeting will have a pile of statistics dumped in his lap, with no time to analyze and digest the facts and figures and ponder a course of action.

As for the directors, even when given plenty of information and enough time to absorb it, too many of them will do little more than skim over the material before a meeting; they are simply too busy with their own full-time jobs. A great many managers, who say they would like nothing better than to beef up their boards of directors, complain that there is a serious shortage of good candidates for directorships—men who have reached that stage of maturity where they can sit apart and judge objectively without meddling in operations, that stage of leisure where they can devote sufficient time to the directorial problems at hand, and that stage of opulence or public-mindedness where they are willing to work for peanuts.

On this last point, it is true that the traditional twenty-dollar goldpiece for attending board meetings long since has been replaced by bigger stipends. Directors' fees often run to $200 or more per meeting these days, and some companies have placed their directors on retainers ranging up to $20,000 a year. Directors of some automobile companies are given free cars—an ingenious form of compensation that does not cost the companies a cent, since after a year of use they can take back the cars and sell them on the secondhand market for more than the manu-facturing cost. But this kind of compensation—even running up to $20,000 or more a year—does not mean much to the high-bracket individual who, because of experience and background, is likely to be in greatest demand as a director.

This shortage, whether real or imagined, means that the known "good" directors are so much in demand that they sometimes are overloaded with directorships. The Ford Foundation's Donald David, who serves on six boards, including those of General Electric, Ford Motor and R. H. Macy, has been invited to serve on many others but has turned them all down for fear of spreading himself too thin. Charles S. Munson, who is chairman of no fewer than three companies (Air Reduction, Cuban Air Products and U.S. Industrial Chemicals) and serves on the boards of ten others, including National Distillers, Consolidated

Edison and Greyhound, shares the same fear. And General Electric's Ralph Cordiner has a flat rule that he will not sit on any board other than his own. When he first became president of G.E., he says there was a steady procession of people in his office asking him to serve on other boards. Many were bankers with whom G.E. does business, and Cordiner had the feeling that they were all afraid he would go on the board of one bank and then favor it with General Electric's trade. "I finally told them I wasn't going to serve on any bank board. I'm sure they all breathed a sigh of relief." As for the other offers, Cordiner turned them down, too. "I don't know where [other directors] find the time," he says. "I think my duty to General Electric's shareholders is to spend all my time on this job."

Despite the signs of atrophy in the board room, there have been some recent encouraging indications that the situation may be improving. Management itself, in many companies, is beginning to be concerned by the scarcity of good men in the board room—as witness the Columbia seminar—and that in itself is a good omen. While many managers have tended in the past to view the board as a necessary evil, there are signs that the pendulum is swinging in the other direction, and that some are now coming to realize how valuable an independent board can be.

One participant in the Columbia seminar talked at length about the differing functions of the top management team (which he called the "cabinet") and of the board of directors. His conclusions are worth quoting:

"You have to have a cabinet. A man who is in a tough executive post has got to be able to call together a group of his associates, his colleagues, his subordinates, and

177

sound out his plans, thrash them out when they are in half-baked form. But, in addition, I believe very strongly that he needs one more step if you are going to have the proper safeguards, and that is the job of proving his point to an independent group that are damn good judges, who have not been participants in the plans, but who stand aside and judge. They interfere in no way with management, but they are judges. I think that if that element is lacking you are always in danger. And I never want to be a chief executive with that element lacking. I have been and I know how damned uncomfortable it is.

"If you've got a program that is going to change the whole face of nature . . . then you've got to sum that up in your own mind and say, 'All right, boys, I may be right and I may be wrong, but here we go.' It is a very different thing if you can walk into a group that are your judges and say, 'Now, gentlemen, this is my program.' Let them attack it, and you defend it, and when you finally come out of there, they say it's all right. . . . Then you go with confidence. But you've got to have that element."

One of the subjects that the Columbia seminar discussed in some detail was the composition of the board. In addition to the company's chief executive, who should serve on it? Should it be made up entirely of "outsiders"— men who have had no working experience with the company, but who because of their careers in other organizations are qualified to judge objectively and bring a fresh viewpoint to whatever problems might arise? Or should it be an all-inside board, composed of men who have always worked for the company and know its operations intimately? Or should there be a balance between the two?

There are advantages and drawbacks in each of the alternatives, and the seminar never did reach agreement on the "ideal" board, since what is good for one company or industry is not necessarily the answer for another. Many utility companies, dealing as they do with a broad segment of the public, think it is absolutely vital for their boards to be composed largely of "outside" directors, chosen not just on the basis of ability, but with an eye to geographical dispersion and diversity of interests as well. A.T. & T., for example, numbers among its nineteen-man board of directors one executive from South Carolina, one from Chicago, one from Kansas City, and one from Massachusetts.

In the oil industry, on the other hand, particularly among the old Standard companies, it is not unusual to find boards composed entirely of insiders. Jersey Standard reasons that its business is so vast and complex that being a board member is a full-time job, and only a man who has grown up in the business can be qualified to handle it. "Of fifteen men on our board," says Jersey's president Rathbone, "there is only one who didn't come up through the ranks. He's a financial man."

The standard criticism of the "inside" director is that because he is beholden to the chief executive, and must live and work every day with the other insiders on the board, he is not likely to criticize the activities of either his boss or his associates. In other words, the argument goes, the "inside" board is likely to become nothing more than a back-scratching operation. But Standard Oil of New Jersey has devised an ingenious solution to this problem. The instant a man is made a Jersey director, he is relieved of all operational responsibilities in the company, in the belief that from that moment on he will no longer regard the chief executive as "the boss." Whether this works in fact is open to question; but it is reasonable to assume that such a basic shift in thinking, if it ever does take place, cannot happen overnight.

The great majority of boards are composed of a combination of insiders and outsiders, and here the danger is that the insiders effectively will run the show, being privy to what is going on in the company and being regarded by the outsiders as the real experts on company affairs. The solution, of course, is to have a greater proportion of outsiders than insiders. "I personally believe," says Donald David, "that a board composed of up to two-thirds outside directors is the best."

For those who share this belief, an encouraging trend has been taking place. In 1938, the National Industrial Conference Board found in a survey that half the companies it studied had boards dominated by outside directors; in 1953, outsider-dominated boards accounted for 54 per cent, and in 1958, 57 per cent. One notable example of a long-time "inside" company that has been taking in outsiders as directors is Ford Motor, which in the last couple of years had added president Harold Boeschenstein of Owens-Corning Fiberglas, president Paul Cabot of Boston's State Street Investment Corp., investment banker Sidney Weinberg, and president Charles H. Kellstadt of Sears, Roebuck. "It's still primarily an inside board at Ford," says one director, "but we're working towards broadening the base." Another example of an inside company turning outward is A. & P., which just recently took on six topflight outside directors.

Considering the minuscule after-tax compensation involved, why should any man at the top be willing to serve as a director? There is prestige involved, of course; and there is the chance that being a director of another company will help a man's own business. (On this point, however, the following quote from the Columbia seminar is pertinent: "We had a time in this country, when I was young, when boards were assembled with people who thought they could make something out of it on the side, when the members of the board went around the barn with inside information, with special contracts or something. That day is pretty well over.") Then, too, there is the sheer fascination of the work. "It's interesting," says Charles Munson. "If you don't have many problems, life is very dull. Also, by serving on other boards you can learn a lot about your own business. The same problems recur."

Beyond this, the fact seems to be that the directorial urge of many men stems from a lofty motivation. Little has been written about directors in the past without at least a passing mention of Wall Street's Sidney James Weinberg, the champion director of them all. This book is no exception. For, by common consent, Weinberg exemplifies the kind of highly motivated individual that every company should have as a director. Not only has Weinberg, a five-foot-four-inch package of realized ambitions, sat on some thirty-five boards in his day—and thirty-one of them all at the same time—but he has managed to find time to apply himself effectively to each and every one of his directorial tasks.

Now in his late sixties, Weinberg recently has been cutting down on his directorships, and at last report could claim only ten or eleven, including Ford Motor, General Electric, General Foods, B. F. Goodrich, Continental Can and National Dairy Products. Yet the demands of these are such that he still has to spend many hours every weekend poring over financial reports and other information concerning his interests. "I love annual reports the way some men do stamps," Weinberg once said.

Why does he work so hard at his directorships? The $50,000 or so that he collects each year in directors' fees is not the reason; 90 per cent of that goes in taxes, anyway. The other fees that he picks up as an adviser, stemming from his many contacts and running into the hundreds of thousands, apparently are not the answer either, since Weinberg turns these over to Goldman, Sachs & Co., the investment banking house of which he is senior partner. A few years ago, Weinberg explained it this way to E. J. Kahn, Jr., of *The New Yorker:* "I regard being a director of a large corporation as a semi-public service. A man in my tax bracket gets nothing out of it except terrific responsibility, and he'd be silly to assume that responsibility unless he looked on it as a public service."

A product of P.S. 13 in Brooklyn, Weinberg got his start in business as a $2-a-week "flower and feather horse" —a delivery boy for a milliner. His first job at Goldman, Sachs was as assistant janitor, with the duties of cleaning out the spittoons and polishing the partners' rubbers on rainy days. Irrepressibly brash and buoyant, he finally caught a partner's eye, took some night courses in finance and soon was impressing his colleagues with a kind of financial and human acumen seldom displayed by a janitorial assistant before or since. As the years passed, Weinberg became sought after not only by the biggest financial interests in the nation, but by the U.S. government as well. A dollar-a-year man during both the Second World War and the Korean War, Weinberg's persuasiveness in luring top businessmen to work in Washington earned him the title of "body snatcher." A few years ago, when the Ford Foundation made its historic public offering of 10.2 million shares of Ford stock, it was Weinberg who worked out all the details and served as the key intermediary among the Ford family, the foundation, the N.Y. Stock Exchange and the Internal Revenue Service.

It may be that Weinberg's diligence as a director stems, in part, from an early experience in his directorial career—the time in 1938 when he and the other directors of McKesson & Robbins were hoodwinked by the swindler Philip Musica, alias F. Donald Coster, who as president bilked the drug company and its shareholders of millions. Not many years before, Weinberg had written what amounted to a creed for directors, which was widely circulated in financial quarters. It was not surprising that, in the investigation that followed the McKesson & Robbins scandal, Weinberg was confronted with his creed and was asked why he had not lived up to it as a director of the drug company. He later wrote in the *Harvard Business Review:* "I pointed out . . . that Moses had brought down the Ten Commandments from Mount Sinai, that we all believed in them, but that unfortunately few of us live in accordance with all of them."

But Weinberg follows the creed today, and spreads the gospel by campaigning for directorial responsibility. For the past few years, he has been plumping especially for mandatory retirement for directors, and for the infusion of young blood in the board room—a campaign that has the hearty approval of such equally exemplary directors as Donald David, sixty-three, and Charles Munson, already seventy. (The fact that General Electric has recently added four men to its board, all under fifty, no doubt reflects the Weinberg philosophy.)

"We directors have got to prepare younger men to take our places," Weinberg told *The New Yorker*. "There ought to be room for them on our boards before they're fifty. I told most of my boards that I would be willing to resign when I reached sixty-five, but I know damn well they'll have to kick me off when I reach seventy"—an event due to take place in 1961. "At that age, nobody ever wants to give up *anything*."

What to do with directors over the age of seventy? Sidney Weinberg has a typically forthright, if somewhat extreme, solution: "Chloroform them!"

# 13.

# MR. EXECUTIVE
# GOES TO
# WASHINGTON

ONE SUNDAY MORNING in December, 1950, General Electric's then president Charles E. Wilson was shaving in his Scarsdale, New York, home, getting ready to go to church, when the maid knocked on the door and announced: "Mr. Wilson, the President wants you on the telephone." "Electric Charlie" (in contra-distinction to General Motors' "Engine Charlie" Wilson) thought it was just another gag by his old friend and neighbor Sidney Weinberg, who was forever calling and announcing himself with the words: "This is the president." Slowly, Wilson wiped the soap from his face and ambled to the phone. "Hello, Sidney," he said, somewhat wearily. "What's on your mind?"

The voice from the other end of the line sounded far away. "This isn't Sidney," it said. "This is Harry Truman." The President wanted Wilson to come to Washington right away; it was a matter of utmost urgency.

Next day, at the White House, Truman explained the problem. The Korean War, then six months old, was not going well; in the President's opinion, as he told Wilson, World War III might not be far away. He wanted Wilson, who had served in Washington during World War II, to come back as the nation's mobilization boss. "What the hell was I to say?" Wilson asked later. "That I couldn't afford to do it, when there might be a war? After all, this country had been pretty good to me." He agreed on the spot, and went to work for the government for 6 or 7 per cent of his G.E. pay.

For Wilson, going back to Washington was almost like going home. But for hundreds of other businessmen who take a government job for the first time, the moment they step off the plane at Washington airport is like entering a new and mysterious world. The very novelty of almost every experience helps to explain why so many business-men have so much trouble adjusting to the routine of public life. And nowhere is the change so great as in the process of making decisions.

From the start of the Industrial Revolution, business has been essentially an autocratic, or at least an authori-tarian, affair. Should a new product be produced? A new man hired or an old one fired? A price cut or a wage rate raised? In the end, it is up to the man at the top to decide —and as long as he is at the top he has the power to make his decisions stick.

In recent years, the absoluteness of this authority has been tempered by a number of developments, some of them already discussed in earlier chapters. The growing complexity of business has tended to make the decision-making process more consultative. The growing power of labor unions has steadily encroached on management's traditional prerogatives, most particularly in the area of deciding how profits should be distributed. The hand of government, increasingly felt in corporate affairs, has awakened many businessmen to the political facts of life, and to the importance of public opinion. In addition, the growing realization among top executives of the corporation's responsibility to the community at large has been a tempering influence.

But basically the autocratic, or authoritarian, system still prevails in industry. The responsibility for a decision rests, in the final analysis, with the chief executive—particularly where the board of directors is ineffective, which as we have seen is so often the case. And the top man's responsibility is backed up with the authority to see that his decisions result in action.

Not so in Washington. Suddenly, instead of being absolute boss, the businessman discovers that in government work, even in a top job, he is surrounded by bosses. And while the responsibility for a decision may still be his, the authority for carrying it out is sharply reduced. "No man in Washington, short of the President himself, possesses the final authority that is possessed by the man at the top of a company," says Inland Steel's former boss Clarence Randall, who has spent much time in government service. "Everything has to be done under committee action. . . . The rightness of your idea must prevail."

Charles Percy, another loyal Chicago Republican who has watched many of his friends and colleagues make the big switch into public life, has this to say: "It's a terrible plunge into an icy bath to jump from business, which is essentially an autocracy, into government, which is a democracy. You sit there and get red, ripe tomatoes thrown at you every day in the week. Businessmen, in their normal lives, are protected from this. You don't get many vice presidents blasting the chief executive officer in the news-papers, and very seldom do you get that kind of abuse even from your competitors. Others in the camera industry may think I'm an s.o.b., but they don't blast it out in the open."

The differences are both big and small. At home in the safe confines of his office, the top man's routine may change from day to day, but every effort is channeled in the direction of getting things done. In Washington, the effort is necessarily dispersed. At home, the chief executive is protected by a battery of public relations men from the members of the press, and when he has some-thing to say he will usually issue it in the form of a press release; it is printed on the financial pages, and that is that. But in Washington, where the press operates on the sound principle that the public business is the public's business, many a businessman comes to feel that he is surrounded by a pack of wolves hungering for his flesh. When he re-fuses to talk to the press, he becomes an object of repor-torial hatred—and when he talks, he may get himself in trouble.

On occasion—most notably in the case of former defense secretary Charles E. Wilson ("Engine Charlie")—the felici-tous phrase that reporters so dearly love has come back to haunt the man, and sometimes in a form quite different from the original. Such was the case in the famous remark, attributed to Wilson in a closed committee hearing, that "what's good for General Motors is good for the country." Actually, it turned out that Wilson had said it just the other way around, but the correct version never caught up with the error.

To be fair to the Washington reporters, however, it

should be said that Wilson had a facility for glibness that often seemed out of place in a time of crisis. When unemployment in the 1957-58 recession was a major national problem, Wilson left the very distinct impression that he thought a good deal of the blame lay with people who lacked the get-up-and-go of "bird dogs," who would not go out and hunt jobs for themselves.

To the ordinary businessman, accustomed to the manners and mores of commerce, the Washington atmosphere is an enigma. In business, the manner in which one man deals with another can be brusque, or even rude; while business manners have improved, some still consider abruptness a sign of a brass-tacks, no-nonsense approach to affairs. But no matter what the manners, there is no backbiting in business, for that simply would not be good business. In government, it is quite the other way round. Manners are impeccable; everyone seems to treat everyone else with disarming deference. But the minute a back is turned, the knives begin to flash. And for many politicians, the most inviting target of all is the back of a businessman, the bigger the better.

Baffled by this unaccustomed state of affairs, some businessmen are quite unable to adjust themselves to the Washington atmosphere, with the result that they offend the sensibilities of the legislators (G.M.'s Wilson used to refer disconcertingly to senators in committee hearings as "you men"); they even get themselves in trouble with their former colleagues in the world of business. There is the case, for example, of one businessman-turned-undersecretary in a major department, who made the mistake of offending a certain businessman with whom he was dealing. The businessman spoke to his senator, the senator began to gun for the undersecretary, and it was months before the official could again perform his job unharassed.

Too many businessmen who go to Washington arrive with too little real understanding of the separate and distinct roles of the legislative and executive branches of the government—the checks and balances that have been built into the system and effectively protect the democratic process, but which at the same time make clear-cut decisions and fast action difficult to achieve. Joseph M. Dodge, the Detroit banker who was President Eisenhower's first budget director, puts it this way: "Too often, the businessman has no comprehension of the obstacles to accomplishment in government—where he has to deal with a board of directors of more than 500 people [the House and the Senate] whom he didn't even help select, and cannot hope to control; where there are no private disputes—they're all public; where you have consistent opposition. The result is that the executive who is used to making plans and having them acted upon finds many frustrations. He must compromise in a way he ordinarily wouldn't, and often must end up with selecting the 'least worst' alternative course of action."

The "outside directors," or Congress, are only part of the unfamiliar situation to which many Washington tyros must adjust themselves; there is also the bothersome matter of inside personnel. In business, an executive has the right, the power and the duty to surround himself with a staff of his own choosing, equipped with the talents the job requires. But in government, more often than not, he must accept the civil service employees who have been there for years before his arrival, and most likely will still be there years after his departure. One cabinet officer in the Truman Administration went to Washington full of plans for a clean sweep of his department. But he was able to get rid of only a handful of people, most of them stenographers.

The civil servants know why a policy was launched six, seven or eight years ago, and may have been instrumental in its inception. Thus, it is hard to change course in Washington, particularly, says Meyer Kestnbaum, a special assistant to President Eisenhower, since the civil servants "are not bowled over just by the appearance of a businessman on the scene." This is not so great a problem for those businessmen, like Clarence Randall, who have been "continuously impressed" by the high calibre of government career people. "You've got to know how to work with them," says Randall. "They won't open out to you unless you treat them as equals." But for the executive who goes to Washington, as many do, with the strong suspicion that the civil service offers a sinecure for a bunch of ne'er-do-wells who "never met a payroll in their lives," the matter of personnel is a particular source of frustration Socony Mobil's Albert Nickerson, who put in a year with the War Manpower Commission, concludes: "Some businessmen think that government is not properly motivated. They don't realize that government is a different kind of animal, and they don't realize that government is filled with people who have the desire to serve. These people are motivated differently; they do a good job just for the sake of doing a good job."

As far as the government is concerned, one major problem is the difficulty in recruiting younger men from industry. The younger executives entertain the fear, with reason, that a year or two of Washington work will take them out of the main stream of corporate advancement, and when they return to their companies others will have surged into the lead. And older men, of course, tend to be more set in their ways and less able to make the switch to a life of compromise, or to see why things must be done differently in Washington. (After a stormy stint as a top man in a big government agency, one automobile executive returned to industry with the comment, "We didn't learn a thing; it's just the same as running a business.") When Ralph Cordiner was with the War Production Board, he was only forty-two. "I'm now fifty-eight," he said not long ago, "and I don't think I'd be as good today as I was at forty-two. I was more pliable then." Furthermore, older men often lack the plain physical stamina that the Washington life demands. The long hours traveling or in the office, followed by the long hours of official socializing, once caused hard-working "Engine Charlie" Wilson to complain: "It isn't the first shift that gets you down, it's the second."

Another problem for the government is to persuade the top men to stay away from their companies for more than a couple of years. One aircraft producer says: "The guy goes down to Washington on the first of May, we'll say. It takes him two or three months to get briefed on what goes on and how to get things done. Finally, from August to February he works—and then from February to May he spends most of his time looking at the calendar, counting the days until he can go home, and wondering who he should have as a successor." Former Air Force Secretary Thomas K. Finletter, who has long argued for a system under which each department would have a permanent, professional undersecretary, estimates that it takes at least a year and a half to learn the ins and outs of a major Washington job—"and probably three years before you're making a real contribution."

In view of all these weaknesses in the system, and in the average businessman's preparation for government work, how effective is Mr. Executive when he goes to Washington? To hear some of his peers in industry talk, not very. "The businessman in Washington has turned out to be a real letdown," says a top West Coast industrialist. "We've all been let down. The American businessman who has gone to Washington has been a child in the hands of the politicians. They've made monkeys out of themselves and the rest of us." What is needed? Shell Oil's president H. S. M. Burns says crisply: "Better government people in government, not businessmen in government."

Nevertheless, long-time government officials and members of the Washington press corps who are in a position to judge are by no means agreed that businessmen make bad public servants. Their view seems to be that businessmen are no better, nor any worse, than any other group: it all depends on the man, and generalizations are likely to be false. It might be supposed, for instance, that the businessman would be most effective in carrying out a specific government job, and least effective in the area of formulating national policy. Yet there have been businessmen who have failed miserably at performing specific, well-defined tasks, and others who have proved themselves brilliant in the making of policy. Clarence Randall, who now is the presidential assistant for foreign economic affairs, explains some of the techniques for formulating policy: "We get together members of the various departments concerned, at a meeting, say, at four in the afternoon. At ten minutes to five, after everybody has talked about the problem, a consensus is reached, and I say, 'Gentlemen, there is a consensus as follows—' and that then becomes government policy, not because I say so,

but because there is agreement. . . . I have never decided anything in Washington, but everything gets decided under that kind of leadership. . . . 'Compromise'
is a little too strong a word. It's more a matter of reaching
a common denominator of thoughts. And mark you, there's
great strength behind a program once it is decided in this
way, because such an agreement has been reached by all
the interested parties."

   Businessmen like Randall and "Electric Charlie" Wilson owe much of their Washington success to their ability
to indulge in the give and take of government, and thus
lead men to a meeting of minds. But there have been
other executives, not known for such diplomatic niceties,
who have also left their marks as government officials who
can get things done. One such was Chrysler's long-time
boss, K. T. Keller. A production man and engineer, Keller
took his lumps for years on the subject of Chrysler styling,
which lagged behind the big postwar trend to lower,
longer cars; many held him responsible, in large part,
for Chrysler's dwindling share of the automobile market.
Recently, looking back on all that criticism, Keller passed
it off philosophically. "If you're the chief executive," he
said, "you get more blame than you deserve, and you
also get more credit than you deserve when things go
right. If you want one—and who doesn't—you've got to
accept the other, too."
   In 1950 Keller, like G.E.'s Wilson, was called to Washington by Harry Truman, who appointed him the nation's
missiles "czar." By the time he stepped down in 1954,
Keller was being blamed in some quarters for having con-
centrated too much on production, and not enough on

developing weapons of the future. But he could also claim the credit for getting the whole missiles program off the ground—and the first generation of missiles in the air. This was something which many military experts still consider a fantastic achievement; and as far as Keller is concerned, it was the job he was hired to do. "If I take this job," he told the President, "I want to do it my own way." And so he did.

For six weeks Keller studied the state of the missile art. He found that there were four thousand people working on the program in the government, and another eleven thousand in such contracting firms as Bell Aircraft, Convair and Hughes Aircraft, scattered around the country. "I decided this was a pretty big organization to pull together in one place," Keller said; instead, he put together a staff of only nine people, including two secretaries and one sergeant to keep the security files, and took to the road—or, more accurately, the air. In one year he logged 150,000 miles in a military Constellation, inspecting missile activities and installations all over the U.S. and in the Caribbean. "The first time round," he said later, "they're scared of you; on the second round you get something done. Finally, we broke the missiles loose and made them go."

Keller talks as a production man of the way the Pentagon is structured: "You've got 32,000 people there, of whom 5,000 are busy really working with contractors, or are scientists actually getting things done. I call this the production side. The other 27,000 are on the policy side, and to get a meeting of minds out of these people, and to get a decision, is a pretty tough job."

Keller knocked heads together, froze designs and

speeded things along. At one point, there was considerable trouble with a certain missile that was forever misfiring or blowing up in the air. The scientists blamed the production men, the production men blamed the men on the firing line, and the men on the firing line, in turn, blamed everyone else. Keller spent a day with each group, hearing them out. Then he called them all to Washington for a meeting, and when they started pointing fingers at one another again, he told them sharply: "If you people don't get this thing working in six weeks, I'm going to the President and tell him that we should cancel the whole project." It took only four weeks, Keller says, to work the bugs out and get the missile flying properly.

Sometimes, it was a matter of moving slowly—as Keller says, "Sometimes you ought to sit back like a Pennsylvania Dutchman and wait for a break; let time work for you." One such case had to do with a new guidance principle that led a Navy admiral to request sixteen entirely new missiles incorporating the breakthrough. To press his point, the admiral brought fourteen commanders and four lieutenant commanders to a meeting with Keller. "Why not apply this new principle to missiles already proved out?" Keller asked. That started a three-hour discussion of electronics, at the end of which Keller repeated his question—"and off they went again for another three hours." Keller left for dinner, and next morning, when he ran into the admiral in the hall, he asked: "Did you get the fleet back to port last night without any casualties? I've never seen such a naval maneuver in my life!"

For a week, Keller did nothing about the matter, and finally the admiral came to see him—alone. "They took the whole goddamn program we wanted 'em to take in the first place," Keller says; the new guidance principle was applied to missiles already proved out. The waiting game, in short, had worked.

More often, however, Keller's method was to move fast. One day in the fall of 1950, he visited the Bell Laboratories to check the progress of the Nike-Ajax missile. On the wall a big chart showed that the first test of the missile was not scheduled until the spring of 1955. "I was sick at my stomach," Keller recalls. He asked to tour the lab, and as the inspection party made its rounds, Keller hung back to talk to a young man running an electronic machine that simulated a missile's flight. He was trying to find out, he told Keller, whether the missile would tumble at seventy thousand feet and thirty-five miles out. It had already been proved out, on the flight simulator, for twenty-five miles and sixty thousand feet—"but they've just moved the specifications up on us, and there's hell to pay."

With that nugget stowed away, Keller finished the inspection tour. At a conference of about forty scientists, production men and military officers later in the day, he started asking general questions ("I knew I couldn't expose this kid, or it would be his neck"), and finally drew out the fact that the specifications had just been moved up. Keller ordered that the specifications be frozen. The result was that Nike-Ajax missiles were being installed around the country not in the spring of 1955, as had been anticipated, but in the summer of 1953.

Travel, they say, is broadening, and it is probably true that few excursions are more broadening for a businessman than a trip to Washington. Wrapped up as they are in their own affairs, many businessmen still tend to take a narrow approach to the world around them, and to assume that all that is needed in Washington is "a good, sound, businesslike way of doing things." But a tour of duty in the capital can be an eye-opening experience, a formidable reminder that the government there is concerned not alone with 175 million people in the United States, but with the entire free world. "The businessman," says Clarence Randall, "is convinced that if we would only bring a good, clean business approach to government, all would be well. But then he finds out why his answers didn't work when others tried them—and very often it's because there is a law against that particular solution." Joseph Dodge agrees: "After serving in Washington, businessmen tend to modify their critical attitude of all that goes on there; they tend not to think any more that they have all the answers."

The healthy exposure of businessmen to Washington got its first massive push during World War II, when droves of executives swarmed into the emergency wartime boards and agencies. For many of them, accustomed to years of New Deal blasts against business, this served as a great awakening. Suddenly they realized that government—even a Democratic administration—is not necessarily evil in itself, and that there can be great satisfaction in serving the interests of an entire people.

The years since the Second World War have seen a continuing influx of businessmen to Washington, as government has continued to grow and as business itself has become more closely interdependent with government, both in national and international affairs. Time and again, companies are asked to lend their middle management people to one government agency or another, for a few months at a time. And as this influx has continued, the middle managers and the companies that employ them have come more and more to realize that time in Washington, far from being an interruption in a corporate career, can prove to be a valuable experience and a plus factor in a man's Personnel dossier. Just as many of the men now at the top had wartime experience in Washington, so it is likely that many of the men at the top ten or fifteen years from now will have had exposure to the workings of the federal government.

Even before World War II brought businessmen to Washington in large numbers, another influence had been affording similar exposure to a more limited group—the men at the very top—ever since 1933. This was the Business Advisory Council, established at the urging of Sidney Weinberg, among others, by Daniel C. Roper, then Roosevelt's Secretary of Commerce. This sixty-man group of top executives has probably done as much as any other single influence to expose the men at the very pinnacle of U.S. industry to each other and to the world. Its first chairman was Gerard Swope, then president of General Electric, and he has been succeeded by such top men as R. R. Deupree of Procter & Gamble, Thomas B. McCabe of Scott Paper (he was chairman of the Federal Reserve under Truman), John L. Collyer of Goodrich, Harold Boeschenstein of Owens-Corning Fiberglas, and Eugene Holman of Jersey Standard. Stephen D. Bechtel, the San Francisco construction-engineer, became B.A.C. chairman in January, 1958.

The B.A.C. usually meets six times a year, often at such resorts as Hot Springs, Virginia, and Sea Island, Georgia, and at its sessions the top men spend hours talking among themselves and with government officials about the economic situation in the nation and the world. In addition to the formal meetings, there are black tie dinners and rounds of golf where the conversations continue for hours more. Reporters are not welcome to the closed sessions, but they are tolerated to the extent that in the past few years the B.A.C. has agreed to hold press briefings after each meeting.

How much good the government gets from the B.A.C.'s advice is hard to say. At the beginning of the 1957-58 recession, the council cautioned against injecting any big public works program into the economy. As the performance of the economy later showed, the B.A.C. was right—but for the wrong reasons. The council opposed public works, in part because the members foresaw no more than a 1 per cent decline in the U.S. economy. Actually, output dipped a total of 14 per cent during the recession, but the economy was strong enough to snap back much faster than most people, including the B.A.C., would have believed possible.

But as a means of keeping in touch with industry, during Democratic and Republican administrations alike, the B.A.C. has been invaluable. It has also served as a sort of training ground from which Washington has been able to recruit top men with broad views and interests. Among council members who have moved in and out of top government jobs over the years are former Secretary of the Treasury George Humphrey, Defense Secretary Neil McElroy, both Charlie Wilsons, Sidney Weinberg, Clarence Randall, Paul G. Hoffman, former Army Secretary Robert T. Stevens, Averell Harriman, Eric Johnston, John W. Snyder, John Hay Whitney, and Philip D. Reed.

To the question of how good a public servant the present-day top businessman can be, the answer seems to be mixed, as we have seen. But how good a public servant will the business community be turning out in the future? There are strong reasons to believe that business—particularly big business—will be turning out better and better prospective material in the years to come, for the dual reason that (1) business itself has been becoming more and more like government in size, complexity, and the decision-making process, and (2) more and more rising young executives are putting in time in Washington as a normal part of their careers.

It will probably never be possible to pluck a top businessman from his company and place him in government with full assurance that he is the best man for the job— any more than such a sure thing can be found among lawyers or doctors or professors. But the chances are that as business becomes ever more consultative, and businessmen become ever more aware of their varying publics—their stockholders, suppliers, customers, and the American people at large—the large corporation will tend more and more to supply the kind of fertile soil from which good public servants are most likely to spring.

Franklin D. Roosevelt used to remark to "Electric Charlie" Wilson, from time to time, that "some of these businessmen who come to Washington grow in the job; others just swell." There is hope that more and more of them who go to Washington in the future will arrive already full-grown, or well on their way.

# 14.

# POLITICS:
# TOGETHER
# WE STAND?

IN THE SUMMER of 1958—months before the Democratic party, with a strong assist from organized labor, won its greatest electoral victory in years—the senior vice president of Gulf Oil dispatched a letter to all the employees and shareholders of the corporation. His message did not have to do with a newly discovered oil field, nor with company profits, nor a change in personnel. The subject was politics, and the language was tough. "For many years," wrote vice president Archie Gray, "Gulf, together with most other American corporations, has been so busily engaged in business activities that politics has been ignored. [But] whether we want to be there or not, Gulf, and every other American corporation is in politics, up to its ears in politics, and we must either start swimming, or drown. . . . Labor's political power must now be opposed by a matching force. . . . If our free, competitive institutions are to be preserved from destruction by the unholy combination of predatory gangsterism and crackpot socialism that is thriving and expanding under labor's Congressional benevolence, then business has no choice." Gray concluded that business, like labor, must climb into the political ring and start swinging—"or throw in the towel."

When Gray let loose his blast, many of the nation's top businessmen were already agreed that "something had to be done" to get their point of view across more effectively to the American voting public. A couple of months later, when the election returns showed how effective organized labor had been in turning out the vote for its favored candidates, hundreds more came to the same conclusion.

But beyond the broad generalities of free enterprise, what *is* the business point of view? Most of the men at the top of the biggest U.S. corporations are Republicans, but their Republicanism encompasses a broad diversity of opinion. "Businessmen range from reactionary to ultra-liberal," says Meyer Kestnbaum, who places himself in the liberal ranks. "It's hard to be sure that the business community possesses views that correspond with the gospel. A lot of business people have views that I don't subscribe to." Kestnbaum is one who thinks that "we've got to face bigger government in a more complicated world. Many reactionary Republicans fall off at this first turn. They won't face the implications of a population of 175 million and a nation with great responsibilities in the world. . . . I'm opposed to the doctrinaire view that everything was fine when the national budget was $15 billion. Nevertheless, I put great importance on performing the functions of government with efficiency and economy."

It is not hard today to detect a schism among the top Republican businessmen—the same sort of split that resulted in the Taft-Eisenhower battle of 1952, and that bids fair to repeat itself in a Nixon-Rockefeller fight in 1960. Some political pundits have concluded that between Nixon and Rockefeller there is no real ideological gap, but America's top executives are not at all persuaded. Some of the top men favor Rockefeller. National Gypsum's Melvin Baker says: "The liberal and progressive movement is the main political movement in America. . . . The liberal tradition is getting stronger and unless the Republicans come up with more men like Nelson Rockefeller, we will be in serious trouble." Others favor Nixon. Fred Kappel of A.T. & T., who puts himself "somewhere between" an Eisenhower Republican and a Nixon Republican, has this to say of Rockefeller: "Some of the things he's said make no sense to me." And Blaw-Knox's president Cordes Snyder says: "I'm for Dick Nixon. He's political enough, and he's not one of these old-fashioned reactionaries. I don't see much difference between Harriman and Rockefeller." Still others like both Nixon and Rockefeller.

This sampling of divergent views shows how hard it is to say what American business is *for;* it is less difficult, however, to state what business is against, or at least what it has been against in the past. For years, the spokesmen of business cried out vaguely (and in vain) *against* the New Deal, *against* the Fair Deal, *against* the specter of "creeping socialism," *against* the "welfare state," *against* high government spending and budgetary deficits, *against* the growing power of organized labor. Long before that, during the Bryan-McKinley campaign of 1896, some factory owners went so far as to insert notices in their employees' pay envelopes, advising: "If Bryan is elected, do not come back to work. The plant will be closed."

But what was business *for?* Some cynics have been moved to recall—unfairly, let it be said—the testimony of Jay Gould, who told the New York State Legislature in 1873 about his political activities in behalf of the Erie Railroad: "In a Republican district, I was a Republican; in a Democratic district I was a Democrat; in a doubtful district I was doubtful; but I was always for Erie!"

Businessmen today are not guilty of such triplicity, of course. More often, they have chosen to stay on the political sidelines. Recalling the adverse effects to business of corporate politicking in the past—such as the trust-busting era that marked the turn of the century and, later, the web of regulatory and competing government agencies that was cast about business by the New Deal—many executives decided to keep quiet or, at most, to let themselves be heard through trade and industry associations that pretended to speak for the many but often as not ended up saying little or nothing for the few. And when individual businessmen *have* spoken out in the past generation, many have done so from a narrow viewpoint, pounding the table in behalf of special interests. "Too often," commented Crawford Greenewalt not long ago, "I am afraid that businessmen approach this delicate area [of politics] more in anger than in reason, with an atmosphere of conflict about them."

Over the years, no business organization has been more vocal politically than the National Association of Manufacturers—and in the opinion even of many of its own members, particularly its big business members, it has not done much to help the cause of business. N.A.M. used to be dominated by big business. But now, while big business is still represented on the board, it no longer dominates the N.A.M. In fact many men who in another day might have been expected to be the guiding spirits of N.A.M. are now its severest critics. "It has stereotyped positions that are inflexible; it has a reputation for being reactionary and rigid," is the way Joseph Block of Inland Steel puts it. "The N.A.M. has the curse of death on it," says Edward Hanley of Allegheny Ludlum. Blaw-Knox's president Snyder says: "Their program doesn't appeal to the people they're trying to impress. It's a mutual admiration society. I used to go to all the meetings and all that, but not any more. I probably ought to tell them to go to hell." In the opinion of Rexall's Justin Dart, the N.A.M. is "a negative influence. I'm completely out of sympathy with it. They want to turn the goddamn clock back. They represent coal-black reaction." A big Midwest industrialist adds: "They're just a bunch of top-drawer guys in their ivory tower, stewing in their own juice and issuing feudal and futile pronouncements. They do nothing but talk to themselves."

This unfortunate reputation is largely, but not entirely, of N.A.M.'s own making. It dates back to the thirties, when the Roosevelt Administration seized upon the association as a whipping boy—and when (or so it seems in retrospect) the N.A.M. was fairly inviting the lash. The temper of the times was such that many top businessmen in those days thought, with some reason, that they were fighting for their very lives. The idea of Social Security was anathema; surely this radical new idea would obliterate the individual incentive that built the country. To these men, at least, the New Deal's regulatory legislation seemed sure to wipe out free enterprise.

The result was that out of thirty-eight New Deal measures the N.A.M. opposed no fewer than thirty-one, including Social Security, Reciprocal Trade, Emergency Work Relief, the Securities Exchange Act and the Public Utility Holding Company Act. N.A.M. was so busy opposing things in those days that it had little time to draw up a real program of its own to support. Texas Instruments' Erik Jonsson reflects the view of many businessmen today —and of many of N.A.M.'s own members—when he says: "The N.A.M. has a consistent negative attitude, and people have come to identify it with 'No.'"

In recent years, N.A.M. has made efforts to change this public image of itself.* The association has invited college students and even labor leaders to sit in on some of its sessions. In 1957, an N.A.M. staff memo urged: "It is time for us to drop the defensive position and become positive. Our concern can no longer end with the welfare of the stockholders. To insure the well-being of our individual businesses, we must contribute to the well-being of the whole business system. Our job used to be to make a profit. Now it is to make the system run fully." To this end, N.A.M. has an extensive educational program that distributes material to schools all over the country, explaining the workings of free enterprise, and an active woman's division to rally the distaff members to the cause of capitalism. "I decided to serve on the board of directors of N.A.M.," says U.S. Rubber's president John W. McGovern,

---

* Indeed, the fact seems to be that the public thinks better of the N.A.M. than most N.A.M. members themselves suspect. In April, 1959, Opinion Research Corp. interviewed 598 executives of N.A.M. member companies and found that while 82 per cent agreed with most positions N.A.M. takes on national affairs, the members believed that only 20 per cent of the public views the association favorably. Actually, another O.P.R. survey showed that 58 per cent of the public views N.A.M. favorably.

"because I feel the association has an opportunity to make our business better understood and to show how it operates in the interest of all the citizens who have a stake in it."

Yet sometimes in the past, just when the N.A.M. seemed to be moving ahead, it has reverted to its old posture of defense. The most notable recent example had to do with a 1959 radio broadcast by Edward R. Murrow, which explored the use of commercial sex in business, as a means of making friends and influencing customers. The program left the distinct impression that industry was shot through with part-time panders—and N.A.M. quickly leaped to the defense of business virtue. Many thought that its method of retaliation was reminiscent of Joe Mc-Carthy at his most insinuating. N.A.M. issued a statement to the press charging that labor unions had persuaded Murrow to put on the show in order to take the heat off labor in the McClellan Committee hearings. When asked later if N.A.M. had proof of this charge, the association's executive vice president (and former president), Charles R. Sligh, Jr., replied: "We can't prove that, but it seemed like a logical reason."

What is the matter with N.A.M.?

In the opinion of many members, the association is simply too big—a total membership of more than 22,000, represented by a board of 170 which can approve new policies only with a two-thirds majority. The result, these members say, is that resolutions are compromised to the point of meaninglessness, and on some issues—most notably tariffs—the N.A.M. is unable to take any stand at all.

Others charge that N.A.M. has been taken over by its staff of 397—and in fact the press release concerning Murrow was a staff-inspired idea, executed without the approval of the board or of the president. But as N.A.M.'s president Stanley Hope quite logically points out, if it is true that the association has been taken over by its staff, the members have no one to blame but themselves.

Still others say that N.A.M. is run by small businessmen who tend to have a less sophisticated and worldly-wise approach to public affairs than do their bigger brethren, who enjoy a far greater exposure to each other, to Washington, and to the world. The belief that N.A.M. is dominated by small business seems to be supported by the fact that more than 80 per cent of its members employ fewer than five hundred employees—but on the other hand the association's current president, Stanley Hope, is a graduate of Esso Standard, of which he was president until 1958, and a number of members of the board similarly come from big business.

Whatever has been the matter with N.A.M. in the past, president Hope resolved to change. He believes that N.A.M. has not for a long time been the stodgy, hidebound organization it once was; the members simply are not aware of the changes that have taken place. "Our problem has been poor communications," he says. "My policy is to try to lead the N.A.M. to a more reasonable approach. I want to express the view of reasonableness. We have to choose our language carefully. I assumed that the members knew how good we were. Instead, they knew how bad we are."

In any case, it was evident to many businessmen in the fall of 1958 that N.A.M. was not the best medium through which to express themselves politically. For the same reasons, if to a lesser degree, the same was true of the U.S. Chamber of Commerce. In fact, the more thoughtful minds in the business community were becoming aware of a deep-seated sociological problem that called for far more than the standard speeches, publicity handouts and viewings-with-alarm. This problem, which goes to the very core of the democratic system, has to do with the state of mind of what, for lack of a better phrase, sociologists call the middle class.

In generations past, the middle class has provided the backbone of political activity in the U.S., and the balance weight that kept the political pendulum swinging back toward center, from right or left. In recent years a new middle class—comprising millions of white-collar workers and middle management people—has been multiplying fast, as a result of rapidly advancing industrialization, the consequent upgrading of jobs, and the explosive growth of the "service industries," ranging from travel to dry cleaning. But at the same time that it has been growing numerically, the new middle class seems to have been shrinking in political importance. And the apparent reason is even more disturbing than the fact itself: The new middle class has lost interest.

Sociologist David Riesman puts it one way—the middle class, he says, is composed more and more of "political consumers," people willing to *consume* what is given to them in politics but unwilling to help *produce* the product as they have in the past. Andrew Hacker, an assistant professor of government at Cornell, expresses the same thought: "Their political participation is confined, by and large, to voting in the more publicized elections. . . . Yet the vote, it should not be necessary to say, is the barest minimum of political participation, and apart from the presidential contests—staged, staffed and directed, it may be said, by people other than themselves—the middle class leaves itself out of political activity. They look upon politics as news to be consumed, a drama to be watched. They have none of the sense of political commitment which was second nature to the middle class of previous generations."

No one can be precisely sure of the reasons for this basic change of attitude, but Hacker explored one fascinating possibility in a study made under the auspices of the Fund for the Republic. In part, at least, he blames the modern corporation for the new political apathy. "One of the attributes of this emerging middle class," he wrote, "is its transiency. Uprooted from the small town and the urban slum, these 'new people' are prepared to sever their old attachments and to move to new locations. Almost gypsy-like in their willingness to pursue their careers in whatever part of the country their corporate employer sends them to, they become truly national in their citizenship. A man who once claimed Flatbush or Fayetteville as his home now looks upon the whole country as his residence. The question arises: Is it possible to be a citizen of a huge nation in any but the most formal of senses? Can national citizenship substitute for a concept which has always had its focus in a local area?" In Hacker's opinion, and in the opinion of many other political scientists, the answer is clearly in the negative. The fact is that for many citizens the corporation has replaced the local community as the focal point of their existence.

Whatever the reasons, political apathy has taken hold. And in the cold, gray, Republican dawn after the 1958 election, many businessmen decided it was high time to replace middle-class apathy with middle-class action. Some of the top men, in their businesslike way, felt like grasping their middle managers by the lapels, and wrestling them into politics—Republican politics, of course. But wiser minds counseled otherwise. It is one thing, these men said, to consider civic and charitable activities as little more than an extension of the normal corporate job; but it is quite another to so consider politics. The head of a department, for instance, can turn over a Community Chest campaign to a subordinate with hardly a second thought—everyone is for the Community Chest. But the same man cannot very well turn over the job of raising money for the Republican cause to a subordinate who may be a Democrat.

The whole concept of the corporation or its management taking a partisan political stand is shot through with practical and ethical questions, not the least of which is the matter of law.

The key Federal law governing corporate (and labor) political activity is Section 313 of the Federal Corrupt Practices Act. This section states, apparently plainly, that "it is unlawful . . . for any corporation whatever, or any labor organization to make a contribution or expenditure in connection with any [federal] election." But how much does that really mean? Nobody knows. Organized labor has successfully skirted, or ignored, the apparent intent of the law through the establishment of the AFL-CIO Committee on Political Education (COPE) to handle its politicking (just an educational activity, labor insists). And when the Justice Department has tried to enforce Section 313, it has been to no avail. In the opinion of some experts, in fact, the Section might well be declared unconstitutional, if tested, as an infringement on the right of free speech guaranteed by the First Amendment.

To try to unsnarl some of the legalities involved, a group of Pittsburgh's major companies pooled their legal talent in 1958 for a study of the pertinent laws, state by state. What they discovered was that the law says many different things in many different places, and that while certain political acts by corporations are forbidden by state laws, many of these laws would be declared unconstitutional if properly tested. Here are some of the major findings:

1. Corporate contributions to candidates or to their committees, to political parties or to persons for aid to candidates or parties, would violate the Federal Corrupt Practices Act, the Hatch Act, and the laws of thirty-five states. On the other hand, contributions to support *measures* up for a vote do not come under Federal law. While such contributions do violate the laws of twenty-five states, the lawyers concluded that these laws would probably be ruled unconstitutional if properly tested.

2. Assignment of a corporation's employees to assist a candidate or his committee, or a political party, falls in the gray area under Federal law and under the laws of twelve states; it would violate the laws of fifteen states.

3. Lending or giving a candidate or his party such things as company transportation, office space or printing facilities falls in the gray area under Federal law; it violates the laws of twenty states.

4. The use of corporate funds for "inside" communications—to employees, stockholders or customers—in support of candidates, parties or measures to be voted on, seems to be legal under Federal law but violates the laws of nineteen states; these, however would probably be declared unconstitutional if properly tested.

5. The use of corporate funds for "outside" communica-

tions—to the public at large—is banned by Federal law when it is in support of candidates or their parties. Such expenditures are probably legal, however, when made in support of *measures*.

Beyond the legalities involved, there are many other ramifications to political activity by the corporation or its top man. For one thing, what about employee reaction? If an employer comes out four-square for a candidate or a party, is there not an implicit threat, however often or vigorously denied, that employees who take an opposite stand are not exactly furthering their corporate careers? And what of the stockholders, suppliers and customers— particularly when a company's biggest customer happens to be, as is often the case, the government itself? Edgar Kaiser, for one, believes that his companies have no place in politics. "We work for both Democrats and Republicans, and we bend over backwards not to influence people," he says. Because of their big government contracts, many aircraft companies similarly shun politics.

The government is not the only customer that can stir up trouble for the politically-minded corporation. The Glidden Co.'s Dwight Joyce, for example, will not soon forget the 1958 campaign, when he was the lone dissenter in the local Chamber of Commerce on the advisability of supporting the right-to-work amendment in Ohio—the measure which many credit for the Republicans' disaster in Ohio that year. Joyce was opposed to the amendment for the good and sufficient reason that Glidden has had more labor troubles in right-to-work states than in others where its plants are located. "I was careful not to be quoted on this stand publicly," Joyce says. "This is a big corporation, owned by twenty-five thousand stockholders, and it has

eight thousand employees. Our feeling is that the corporation is a soulless body that should not take a stand on political issues." But Joyce's silence was to no avail. In an un-
guarded moment, one of his underlings let slip to the press
the boss's views on right-to-work, and within hours there
was an avalanche of angry phone calls and telegrams from
Glidden customers, threatening to cancel orders if that sort
of nonsense continued.

Against this one specific instance of customer pressure,
however, it should be noted that other politically active
businessmen have run into nothing of the sort. Few have
been more active than Charles Percy in Republican politics. "Never once have I seen a 'secondary boycott' of our
products as a result of my Republicanism or anything
else," he says. "Schools use our equipment a great deal,
and never once has the Democratic administration of
Chicago said it wouldn't buy Bell & Howell equipment because I'm a Republican."

There is another practical obstacle to a corporation's
taking a partisan political stand. In the words of Arnold H.
Maremont, chairman of Allied Paper, "if a business organization enters the political arena, who chooses the party
which will be favored by its support? The directors, the
shareholders, the chairman of the board? Where does it
find the authority to use shareholders' money for such purposes?" Crawford Greenewalt makes the same point: "I
could never get up and say, 'This is what du Pont thinks'
on a given political issue. It may be what I think. But what
is du Pont—or, for that matter, any other corporation?
It's a slice of humanity—in our case a slice of eighty-five
thousand people."

Faced with all these unanswered and unanswerable

questions, many top businessmen have come to believe that while it is all right for executives or anyone else in a company to take a partisan political stand they should do so as individuals—and the boss should make it clear that he is talking as a private citizen, not as the boss. (Whether he can convincingly compartmentalize himself in this fashion, however, is wide open to question.) As for the corporation itself, these people have concluded that its role in politics should be confined strictly to nonpartisan education and exhortation. "In the last fifty years," says Lockheed's Robert Gross, "corporations have added two new portfolios to their managements—public relations and industrial relations. I say that in the next few years there's got to be a new portfolio—a political vice president. He's got to work his tail off to get people out to vote; he can't be just a Democrat or a Republican."

Many companies that began to think in terms of partisan politics, companies that were planning to enter the political arena with fists flying, have since revised their plans. When Gulf Oil's Archie Gray issued his first pronunciamento in the summer of 1958, it sounded to many as if his company was about to launch an all-out attack on labor's political activities. But in the months that have passed since then, Gulf has worked out a nonpartisan program of political education.

Not only does this kind of approach promise to skirt the pitfalls of partisanship; it is attacking the problem of political apathy at its local roots. As Raymond Moley has written, "The most vital spot to concentrate your energy is not where laws are made but where lawmakers are made." It is not enough merely to thump the tub of publicity "about generalities on good government and issues, and [to bewail] the trend to statism and centralized government." All such generalized appeals, says Moley, "are secondary to personal contacts. Efficient political machines have acted upon this principle for many years. Elections are won on the doorsteps, in the highways and byways, over the farmer's fence, and wherever men and women gather for work, recreation and worship."

Some businessmen have yet to be persuaded that strict nonpartisanship is the only approach for a corporation to take. Yet simple logic argues that the business cause can best be served, not merely by trying to wrestle middle management into the Republican ranks, but by encouraging lively political interest among corporate employees in both major parties. Not only should this tend to increase the voice of conservatism in the Democratic party; it should help counteract the growing tendency to associate Republicanism with big business—a tendency which could ultimately spell the end of the G.O.P. "If businessmen are to achieve maximum effectiveness in politics," Republican national chairman Thurston Morton has said, "they must work toward this goal as citizens rather than as spokesmen for or representatives of just one segment of our national economy." In Morton's opinion, it would be disastrous for the nation and his party alike if a single economic group should grasp unchallenged control of the G.O.P.

(Some cynics in the Republican ranks have another reason for urging corporations to take a nonpartisan approach, particularly as regards their middle managers. "After all," said one man, "if you get ten men active in this group, eight of 'em are going to be Republicans, anyway.")

Can a nonpartisan program of political education really

be made to work? Johnson & Johnson, the surgical dressing company of New Brunswick, New Jersey, has been trying such a plan for eight years now, and is convinced that it not only *can* work, but *does*. The head of J & J, Robert Wood Johnson, in recent years has become associated more and more with the right wing of the Republican party; there is no question whatsoever about his strong partisanship as an individual. Yet since 1951, with his enthusiastic support, Johnson & Johnson has run a political education program for some 2,100 of its white-collar workers on a strictly nonpartisan (and voluntary) basis. On company time, J & J has held numerous panel discussions on politics; it issues bulletins and pamphlets spelling out the need for "fair and just taxation; a sound dollar; integrity in government; support of fundamental constitutional rights; a vigorous two-party system; and a resourceful and respected foreign policy." William Baumer, special assistant to the president and himself a Republican councilman in Westfield, N.J., explains: "Too many companies have the idea of getting into politics as a counter-balance to what labor is doing. We took the positive approach that our program was right in itself."

The J & J program has attracted Democrats and Republicans alike, and the results have been impressive. Shortly after the program started, about twenty people in Johnson & Johnson's white-collar group of 2,100 held appointive or elective political offices in their local communities; in 1959, after eight years, the figure was more than 200, including several state legislators and one state senator (in Texas). Among the twenty towns around J & J's New Brunswick headquarters, there is hardly one that does not have a Johnson & Johnson mayor, or councilman, or member of the school board. Louis F. May, Jr., a supervisor in J & J research, is the Democratic mayor of East Brunswick; Mauro A. Checchio, an executive assistant, is the Republican mayor of Scotch Plains. Harold Fox, a supervisor in manufacturing, is a Republican councilman in Bound Brook; Chester Lambert, another manufacturing supervisor, is a Democratic councilman of Piscataway Township. (When Democrat Lambert first ran for office, he was working as a foreman for three supervisors who were all Republican councilmen in another town; he has since been promoted to supervisor himself.)

Most of these community positions are part-time affairs that do not interfere with the employees' regular J & J jobs. But when an employee wins a state election that takes him off his job for four months, to attend a legislative session, Johnson & Johnson gives him a pat on the back and a leave of absence (without pay).

During the 1958 election, another company took a similar nonpartisan approach in raising money for the two political parties. Dan A. Kimball, a Democrat who served as secretary of the Navy under Truman and now is president of Aerojet-General Corp., the California rocket fuel and engine company, thought up the idea. "We were not trying to mobilize our employees in favor of any law or policy or candidate that would help our industry or our corporation as such," he says. "I think that is dangerous business, and I would have no part of it."

Instead, Kimball urged his employees to learn about the issues, to hear the candidates, to register in the party of their choice, and to vote. He invited such candidates as William F. Knowland, Edmund (Pat) Brown, Clair Engel and Goodwin Knight to speak in Aerojet plants. Then a Good Citizenship Committee headed by two vice presi-

219

dents—one a Democrat, the other a Republican—urged all Aerojet employees to make cash contributions to the candidate or party of their choice. In all, the committee collected $25,000 from 70 per cent of Aerojet's work force of eleven thousand.

At this writing, industry's new interest in politics is still more talk than action, but the movement seems to be growing. Such companies as Ford, General Electric and Johnson & Johnson already have political action programs under way, and others, such as Union Carbide, Johns Manville and the big rubber companies, are developing programs of their own. Even those two famous tub-thumpers, the N.A.M. and the U.S. Chamber of Commerce, now have political education programs that they are urging their members to adopt on a nonpartisan basis.

In his study for the Fund for the Republic, Andrew Hacker concluded: "The corporation has certainly not set out to weaken the foundations of democratic politics, but its growth as the characteristic institution of our time is having this consequence." Now there is hope that the corporation will begin to work for quite the opposite consequence—provided the men at the top remember and respect the vital ingredient of nonpartisanship in the corporation's approach to politics. This does not mean that the corporation cannot or should not take a stand on issues that affect it directly. But as du Pont's Greenewalt has said, "It is the particular, not the general, which is the corporation's proper sphere. It can perform effectively only in defense of its stockholders or employees as such. On many of the larger and more general political questions, there can be no valid corporate position at all." It is fine for executives to take a stand as individuals, Greene-walt continues, but they "should not represent business exclusively any more than labor people should think only in terms of labor and the farmer only in terms of agricul-ture. No business organization escapes the adverse effects of a disrupted agriculture or of an undue penalty on labor. The realities as well as the equities place upon business people, as they place upon all others, the necessity of a broad national viewpoint."

Industry's new program of political education is just be-ginning. But if it is nurtured diligently, administered wisely and guarded carefully, there is the hope that the corporation, instead of weakening the foundations of democracy, as some fear, may cause a great rebirth of political interest among the people who have been Ameri-can democracy's greatest strength in the past.

# 15.

## LOOKING FOR
## THE ANSWERS

*Lunch was over, the visitor from the Kremlin
had spoken, and the Detroit industrialists had peppered
him with sharp and searching questions. Soon Anastas
Mikoyan would be on his way to the West Coast to continue his trip around the country. In some other meetings
with U.S. businessmen he would not find the questioning
quite so pointed. But as the luncheon guests filed out of
the Ford office building that January day in 1959, Mikoyan's son, Sergo, remarked in Russian: "These American
capitalists are tough."*

Sergo was right. The top men of U.S. industry are tough.
In their own field, there is no one like them in the world,
and on the economic battleground, fighting on equal
terms, they can be expected to win. But the trouble is that
in the struggle against international Communism the
terms are not always equal, nor the issues exclusively economic. Beyond that, the challenge these men face does not
spring from international Communism alone, but from
within the American system as well. The nation has
changed vastly since the days of the robber barons, since

Henry Ford's $5 day, even since the days just after World War II. The revolution of rising expectations, now sweeping so much of the rest of the world, has run its course in America, and many of the new expectations have been fulfilled. Now, because he has been so successful a leader of business in a business society, the man at the top of U.S. industry is being asked to assume a new role of leadership—to play the part of philosopher, statesman, politician, moralist, as well.

Whether he should attempt to undertake these awesome new responsibilities is an academic question, for he is being made to do so by the very circumstances that have made the corporation a central force in U.S. life. But how well equipped is he for the job? Perhaps a few of the answers may be discernible in one last look at who he is, what he is like, and what he thinks about the world around him.

The leader of American business is, to begin with, an individual. We have seen how one man follows in his father's footsteps and another strikes out on his own; how one starts from the bottom and another from the top; how one can fall into a job by luck and another grabs the prize after years of careful planning; how one gets up at 4 A.M. to work and how another spends the early-morning hours thinking about the world he lives in; how one hurls himself into civic activities and another shuns the public banquet like the plague; how one regards his high salary as a sort of Nobel Prize while another grumbles at his $100,000 a year.

Yet while they are all so different, in some respects they are the same. Their capacity for work is enormous. They do not work for the money (although they like their pay checks as much as the next man), nor for the power and the glory (although they appreciate these, too), but because it is born within them to consider all business unfinished business.

The man at the top of U.S. business has a transcendent confidence in himself—and while he admits he is not always right, he does not dawdle over past mistakes. If he sees a problem, and often he is the first to see it, he faces it squarely in the sure conviction that it can be solved by him—or someone else. When a European businessman descries a problem, he may conclude that it is one-of-those-things-we-must-put-up-with. The American manager, on the other hand, as Roy Lewis and Rosemary Stewart noted in their book *The Boss*, "constitutionally thinks no problem insoluble; if he cannot find a solution himself he will buy one ready-made from a consultant." Nowadays, more than ever before, he makes his decisions in consultation with others—he must in these complex times—but once a decision is made he carries it through with a bursting enthusiasm that is not found in the average man.

Because his life is dominated by business, he spends lamentably little time with his family (sociologists, in fact, might be well advised to study the long-term effects on a nation when families in the leadership group are fatherless so much of the time). When he moves into non-business spheres of activity, such as politics, he is sometimes at a loss. Yet what is encouraging now is that the very diversity and involvement of modern business have been forcing the business leader to broaden his own involvement and to take a greater interest in the world around him—first in his local community, then in the nation, and now, increasingly, in the world at large. The world, in short, has opened up to the U.S. businessman, and he to the world.

It has been said, quite correctly, that the enthusiasm, vigor and even idealism that the British in the past have devoted to the military, to politics and to the colonial service, Americans have given to business. But what is the purpose of this dedication? Is it all merely a sacrifice at the altar of the "bitch-goddess Success"? Is it true, as New York's Rabbi Louis Finkelstein has charged, that the American businessman "is preoccupied chiefly with gain, coasting on the spiritual momentum of the past . . . propelled by meaningless drives toward materialistic and frequently meaningless goals"?

Many of the men at the top probably could not say themselves, except perhaps to remark, with pragmatic certainty, that "good ethics is good business." Nevertheless, a number of the country's chief business executives do think about the broader moral issues, and worry about what they see and sense around them.

To many of the top men the most distressing trend in American life is a certain lack of purpose and direction, a departure from "the fundamental principles that made this country great." They note with alarm the decreasing emphasis on the individual as master of his fate, and the diminishing of his incentives. They believe, correctly, that the U.S. was built on strong incentives for the individual and for the business company, and they fear that now the trend is against such incentives. One after another, the No. 1 men cite the factors that they think have caused the shift: high taxes that presumably discourage the successful man the most by hitting him the hardest (but which, in fact, have hardly curbed the drive of the top men themselves); labor unions that have made merit almost obsolete as a factor in the pay check (but which, in fact, the bosses recognize as necessary for dealing fairly with large groups of workers); and a government that increasingly concerns itself with the welfare of the individual citizen (but which, in fact, many corporations themselves have emulated and surpassed with more bountiful welfare programs of their own).

These things, many of the top men are convinced, have combined to make Americans work less hard and to lose their *élan vital* (or "vital bounce"). Having never worked for mere security themselves, they cannot understand why anyone else should. And having never had the time to really enjoy the material wealth their work has brought them, they find it hard to comprehend the man who works that he may take it easy in his boat, or car, or plane—or for that matter enjoy any of the other products that the men at the top, ironically, are turning out for him to use. Yet the wise ones realize that, as bosses, they must supply a combination of incentives and security for their workers —and they worry that the corporation itself is a threat to the individual on whom they pin their hopes.

Even such a man as Edward Cole, the small-car individualist of General Motors and as devout a corporation man as can be found, sometimes has second thoughts about his occupation when he thinks about his brother's life. Instead of working for a large corporation, Cole's brother operates a sand and gravel business of his own. Is Ed Cole ever envious of him? "Sometimes I am," he says. "I've often had thoughts of having a business of my own. The one thing I regret about working for a corporation is that I can't leave it to my son or my heirs. My brother has that advantage—and there's a lot of satisfaction of that sort you simply cannot get in a corporate job. There is no compensation for that; the money isn't the thing."

How can the corporation help its employees establish such individual identity? Some managers, as noted in an earlier chapter, have pushed decentralization as the answer; others, like Republic Steel's chairman Charles M. White, an individualist of the old school, have issued pleas for "individual responsibility" among their workers. Most of them agree with General Electric's Ralph Cordiner, who says that the corporation owes its employee "a feeling of belonging—not in any pollyanna sense, but he must feel his work is important. He is entitled to good bosses who recognize the dignity of the individual."

Yet for all the good intentions, the fact remains that much is still to be done—particularly as production-line chores become more and more specific and mechanical, and further and further removed from the final product. How many men in the steel mills or on the automobile assembly lines have found their identity, not in the corporation for which they work, but in the union to which they belong?

Being realists, it is not surprising that the men at the top accept the fact of unionism. But many go far beyond mere acceptance, believing that organized labor has played a major and beneficial role in helping reshape twentieth-century capitalism into a viable system.

On the subject of labor leadership there are widely divergent views. Some are convinced, for example, that Walter Reuther is the greatest menace the nation now confronts—"he wanted to be Mr. Lenin and Mr. Trotsky both, and still does," says one Pittsburgher. But there are many others who admire the man, if grudgingly. "There's too much of the kind of thinking that puts up Reutherism on one side and business on the other," says Cleveland's Dwight Joyce. "I hear this terrible talk about Reuther. I've never met him, but I'm convinced he's no Communist. I am also convinced that he *is* a Socialist, and I can't buy that viewpoint. But I admire him as a man. He believes what he says, and he's a formidable opponent."

Most of the chief executives firmly believe, of course, that there should be corrective legislation to clean up such racket-infested unions as the Teamsters, and many think that the unions have become too strong and should now be made subject to the antitrust laws, as business is. But G.E.'s president Robert Paxton was representative of many in his reason for wanting corrective action soon. "If the correction is delayed too long," he said, "it will have a tendency to be punitive as well as corrective, and this would cause difficulties which could so easily be avoided."

It is in the area of economics, many of the top men believe, that union power poses its greatest threat, being able to impose wage demands that outrun advances in productivity, and which in many cases bear no relation whatever to output per man hour. (In this connection, many top executives roundly damn General Motors' former president Charles Wilson for signing the first wage contract that had a built-in escalator tied to the cost of living.)

To a man, the chief executives consider inflation a looming danger, not just to the U.S. but to the world. In fact, the way some of them talk about inflation is a good indication of the new, enlightened view they are taking of the world. They think of inflation as a much more serious matter than whether Americans can buy the same amount of goods with a dollar tomorrow as they can today. "There's not nearly enough gold around to back the currencies of the free world nowadays," says one, "and the dollar has taken the place of gold. The stability and unity of the entire free world depend on the dollar. If it becomes unstable, God knows what will happen."

And God knows what will happen, many others would add, if the cost of producing American goods continues to rise in relation to the rest of the world.

Here and there, some remnants of isolationism and high tariffism can still be found among the chief executives. One Chicagoan, for example, firmly declares that "the biggest long-range problem facing the nation today is that of minding its own business, making America strong for the Americans, to quit dabbling in the other fellow's affairs." But nowadays the international viewpoint is the rule, not the exception, among the men at the top.

Philip Reed, who has long been one of U.S. industry's leading internationalists, dates his big awakening, as do many others, to World War II (when Reed served with the U.S. economic mission in London). "I was looking at my country from thousands of miles away," he recalls. "They used to ask me, 'Is the U.S. going isolationist again when the war is over?' and I simply couldn't answer." When Reed came back to the U.S. he did his best to spread the gospel of freer trade at every opportunity. "Free trade is like integration," Reed says. "You've always got to keep pushing in at the perimeter, always keep things a little raw around the edges—enough so that you'll get some people mad but not enough so you'll cause a revolt."

As they look at the world around them, many of the No.

1 men conclude that travel and trade are the two surest routes to international understanding (not surprisingly, few feel more strongly about this than international hotelman Conrad Hilton).

Some chief executives would like to see the U.S. lower the bars on trade with China. Northwest Airlines' Donald Nyrop, whose airline no doubt would benefit as a result, is one of these. Visiting Hong Kong on occasion, he has been mightily impressed by the goods flowing into China aboard ships of other nations. "The sooner we begin to realize the potentialities of China—and the opportunities for trade—the better," he says. "Prior to Franklin Roosevelt the policy of the U.S. always was to establish diplomatic relations with any country whose government was stable enough to meet its financial obligations around the world. F.D.R. changed all that, and now it's a matter of whether they're socially acceptable in the family of nations. We ought to go back to the old theory."

Even many of those with strong high-tariff leanings are getting a kind of exposure these days that may tend to lessen their opposition to lowering the trade barriers—an exposure forced on them, paradoxically, by the low production costs abroad which they consider such a threat. Colonel Willard F. Rockwell, an old-school entrepreneur who built up Pittsburgh's Rockwell Manufacturing Co. largely by the sheer force of his personality, damns the foreign giveaway," goddamns "our goddamn bureaucracy" in Washington, and points with a chuckle to a photograph of himself laying bricks onto a structure labeled "Tariff Wall." But Rockwell has concluded that "you've got to think about the world these days"; in fact, he has thought so hard about it that he now has two plants in Germany turning out valves and small engines. He says he pays less than a quarter as much for labor there—and in Germany you get a man "who works harder, is more interested in his work, and does a better job."

Some have feared that Europe's new Common Market will make for a new wave of protectionism in the U.S. But there are few signs of it among the leaders of industry; instead, like Rockwell, more and more of them are setting up plants abroad to compete for markets on equal terms. And obviously any American manufacturer who sets up shop abroad, planning to bring his lower-cost products back into the U.S., is not going to be in favor of high tariffs against himself.

In some areas of America's economic life, the problems seem so basic and firmly rooted that the No. 1 men, so loath to consider anything insoluble, are frankly baffled. They observe the trend to corporate giantism with reservations; some, indeed, would go so far as to have the government break up General Motors and A.T. & T., or at least confine them to more limited areas of operation. Yet the very men who utter such heresies, often as not, are those who complain the most about government interference with their own businesses. Having suggested that "something should be done" about G.M., they interrupt themselves to ask: How can bigness be attacked as such, when in fact it represents the triumph of the very system that has proved more beneficial to more people than any other in the world?

No doubt it was inevitable, the top men quite freely admit, that government would become more involved with business as corporate size and power grew—just as government almost surely will become more and more involved in the affairs of organized labor. They complain that govern-

231

ment is too much in business—but do they really mean it? One executive (it happened to be Louis Wolfson) had this to say: "We render lip service to the ideal of free initiative, but all too often we drift towards reliance on governmental guidance of our destinies. . . . The main difficulty, or so it seems to me, is that while we are eager to enjoy the benefits of free enterprise, we are reluctant to shoulder the responsibilities and the problems inherent in the system. In times of high-level prosperity, we want no part of governmental interference, but the instant a down-trend seems in the offing, we demand to know what the government intends to do to correct this development." One recent example was the successful pressure by domestic oil producers for government quotas on imported oil, in a period of petroleum glut. And there are many others, in the form of subsidies, stockpiling programs and other governmental measures that industry demands in time of stress.

The men at the top talk glowingly of competition, and one gets the impression that they are thinking in terms of dog-eat-dog price-slashing and undercutting, in the grand free-market tradition. Yet in the past many of them have been staunch defenders of Fair Trade laws that make it illegal for one retailer to undercut another. Competition is still very much in evidence, but in some industries price has been replaced by service and quality as a competitive factor—for the simple reason that price competition would bring chaos to the market place.

The thread that runs through all the top men's worries is the fear that somewhere along the line Americans have forgotten their responsibilities as free citizens, that they have come to believe that the democratic system runs itself, and its rewards flow automatically. "Somehow," says one industrialist, "people start taking things for granted. But democracy asks more of its citizens than does any other form of government, and we have to get people to remember this."

If the American people have forgotten such fundamentals, what is the reason? Some say it is because they are not being taught the fundamentals to begin with.* Education is a function which the thoughtful leaders of American business believe can and must be improved, and a heartening number of them have recently interested themselves in matters academic. In part, this is a pragmatic reaction. In the old days, industry could supply its own education to employees on the work bench, but now the needed technical skills are so complex that this is not enough. Beyond this, among many of the top men there is also a refreshing new appreciation of the liberal arts. This stems, no doubt, from their increased exposure to the world of learning through the foundations which so many corporations now support. But it can also be traced to a new and growing belief that leadership in business nowadays must be broadly based.

Education is the kind of problem that money can help

* Lockheed's Robert Gross tells this story to illustrate the ills of U.S. education:

Two little boys in knee pants are standing in the schoolyard during recess when a jet plane whooshes by overhead. "What was that?" asks Jimmy. Answers Johnny: "That was an F-104 . . . no, an F-104 B."

"What kind of an engine does she carry?"

"Why, she's powered by a J-79-dash-7."

"Guess it must get pretty hot in that cockpit at those high speeds."

"Well, it could get up to 185 degrees Fahrenheit, but they have a new Primacool X-13 cooling system with double-action vaporizers, so the pilot doesn't have to worry."

Just then the school bell rings. "Come on," says Johnny with a yawn. "Let's get back inside and start stringing those goddamn beads again."

solve, and here the men at the top are on familiar ground. In 1958, a group of business leaders, including Sidney Weinberg, Pan American's Juan Trippe, Goodrich Rubber's John L. Collyer, C.B.S.'s William S. Paley, and U.S. Steel's former boss Irving S. Olds, formed a committee to urge corporations to contribute more money to the nation's colleges and universities. "Corporations," said Trippe, "are gaining a larger and larger control over the funds of the country. Therefore, it is to them we must look if the great universities with their ever-increasing costs are to keep their standards high, and if they are, in fact, to survive."

Some of the men at the top are the first to attack themselves and their fellow businessmen. "Fundamentally," says Philip Reed, "businessmen haven't been willing to study problems from all sides. . . . We have a tendency to look at things with blinders on. The tendency is to decide whether something is right or wrong only from the standpoint of our own businesses. We've been too negative, too dogmatic, too unrealistic. We haven't been statesmen enough."

But others are the first to say that they have come a long way, and learned a great deal, in the span of a single generation. And so they have. There was a day not so long ago—they used to say "the business of America is business"—when it would have been almost unthinkable for a corporation boss to conclude that his responsibilities extended much beyond the mere making of a profit. But now most of the men at the top believe, and most of their fellow citizens agree, that the profit is merely where their responsibilities begin. The new corporate philosophy is concerned not with profit alone but with people, too, and with the whole community of people that makes up a nation and a world. As Adolf Berle pointed out in *The Twentieth Century Capitalist Revolution,* "the corporation, almost against its will, has been compelled to assume in appreciable part the role of conscience-carrier of twentieth century American society."

One of the most encouraging facts, as the No. 1 men assume this new responsibility, is their own realization—unlike so many of their forebears—that they do not have all the answers. In this fact, indeed, lies the hope that their search for the answers will be spurred all the more.

There are, in the U.S., a limited number of people with the drive and the capacity to be managers in this business society. To them belongs the power, and on them rests the responsibility for the success or failure of the free system that has propelled them to the top. Fortunately, the American system has tended, in recent years at least, to make powerful people good. "Our culture," says Leland Hazard, the Duquesne Club lawyer-philosopher, "has been such that we have quickly civilized the chieftain. We have made him a social being more rapidly and more completely than has any other society anywhere else in the world, at any point in history. What has done it? Christianity and the concept of the worth of the individual. Now the thrilling challenge is whether we can continue to temper the wind of power to the individual lamb."

In the Soviet Union, there is no such concern for the individual lamb. But is it possible that, among Russia's men at the top, there is a greater measure of religious fervor, a greater sense of mission, a greater fire of spirit? This is the true challenge, and the great, unresolved question on whose answer, quite literally, hangs the fate of the entire world.

For as Charles H. Malik, the former foreign minister of Lebanon, has pointed out, the American businessman is judged, and will be judged, by more than his product and his performance; his humanity is at stake.

"Rising above his individual interests to the proper consideration of the common good and soaring even beyond the common good to the spiritual significance of his wondrous material civilization, the businessman can clothe his humanity with a shining new splendor. He will put to shame every culture that ends in boredom, self-sufficiency, and human pride. His spiritualized materialism will have something profound to say and give to all men. He will identify himself with their human state. He will be proud of his business and its achievements, but he will be even prouder of that which is beyond business in his culture. He will say, 'Let others compete with me in material things and let them even excel, but there is one thing in which they cannot excel because they do not know it and are not even seeking it. That is the power and depth and freedom of the spirit in which man is fully himself.'"

These are lofty goals indeed for men so concerned with the business of getting things done. But if America's men at the top can approach these heights—and, granted, they have a fair way to go—it will no longer be a matter of Communism challenging the businessman. Then, as Malik so rightly concluded, it will be the businessman who is challenging Communism.

# INDEX

A & P Company, *see* Great Atlantic & Pacific Tea Company
Abegglen, James, 56
Adams, Avery, 22, 137, 160
Aerojet-General Corporation, 219-220
AFL-CIO Committee on Political Education (COPE), 212
*Age of the Moguls, The,* 134
Air Reduction Company, Inc., 176
Alcoa, *see* Aluminum Company of America
Aldrich, Winthrop, 162
Alexander, Henry, 83, 132, 150
Allegheny Ludlum Steel Corporation, 90, 134, 160, 206
Allen, Frederick Lewis, 89
Allen, Ivan, Jr., 149
Allied Paper Mills, 215
Allyn, Stanley, 32-33, 98, 142, 150
Aluminum Company of America (Alcoa), 93, 128, 159-160, 166-167, 169, 171
Amalgamated Emulsion and Dye Company, 66
American Airlines, Inc., 123, 138
American business, fundamental principles of, 233; *see also* big business; business; businessman; small business
American Cancer Crusade, 150
American Cyanamid Company, 37
American Heritage Foundation, The, 149
American Management Association, 81-90, 99, 115, 141; membership growth of, 85; Ramo's criticism of, 84
American Motors Corporation, 7, 102
American Museum of Natural History, 139, 147
American National Red Cross, 146, 150, 152 n.
American Telephone and Telegraph Company, 5, 16, 30-31, 36, 179, 204; attacks on size of, 231
Antell, Bertel, 107

Appley, Lawrence, 84-88, 141
Aspen Institute for Humanistic Studies, 135-136
Astor, John Jacob, 53
Astor Hotel, N.Y.C., 80-81
Atkinson, Arthur, 31, 54
Atlanta Realty Company, 128
Auchincloss, Samuel S., 19, 116
authority, delegation of, 45, 121
autocracy, in business, 186
automobile industry, 6-7; small cars and, 48, 51
Avco Manufacturing Corporation, 82
Avery, Sewell, 45, 162

background experience, of executives, 31-32
Baker, Melvin H., 43, 127, 150, 204
Bank of America, 116, 132, 137
banks, board membership in, 177
Barr, John A., 45, 136
Baumer, William, 218
Bechtel, Stephen D., 199
Beise, S. Clark, 116, 132, 137
Bell Aircraft Corporation (Bell Helicopter Corporation), 195
Bell & Howell Company, 16, 60-65, 113, 137, 215
Bell Telephone Laboratories, 197
Bendix Aviation Corporation, 100
Berea College, 154
Bergson, Henri, 17
Berle, Adolf A., Jr., 154, 235
Bernstein, Leonard, 18, 157
Bethany College, 152 n., 154
Bethlehem Steel Company, 22
big business, and National Association of Manufacturers, 205-207; Republican party and, 217; threats to "break up," 231
*Big Business Leaders in America,* 56
*Big Change, The,* 89
Big Steel, 8, 159
Black, James B., 33, 43, 127-128
Blaw-Knox Company, 118, 166, 204, 206

237

# INDEX

Bliss, E. W. Company, 100
Block, Joseph, 16, 68, 72, 76, 206
Blough, Roger, 8, 18, 133-134, 139
board member, attendance of
meetings by, 175-176; compensation for, 176, 182; "inside" vs. "outside," 180; replacement of, 172-173; shortcomings of, 175-177; theory vs. fact regarding, 172-184
board of directors, "ideal," 178; ineffectuality of, 174-175; "inside" vs. "outside" members of, 180; as instrument of management, 172 ff.; powers of, 172-184
Boeschenstein, Harold, 180, 199
Bomberault, Abel, 160
Booz, Allen & Hamilton, consultants, 101-102
*Boss, The*, 224
boss's son, delicate position of, 70; pay and promotion of, 71-72; as type, 67, 66-79; son-in-law, 22-23
Boston & Maine Railroad, 23, 141
Boyden, Sid, 104-105, 107, 110-111
Boys' Clubs of America, 150
Boy Scouts of America, 147-148, 151, 152 n.
Branch, Harlee, Jr., 31-32, 43, 47, 124, 130-131, 139
Brandeis University, 152, 154
*Brave New World Revisited*, 135
Breech, Ernest, 100
Breech, Henry, 3
Brook Club, 164
Brown, Edmund (Pat), 219
Bryan-McKinley campaign, 1896, 204
Bullis, Harry, 28, 134
bureaucracy, Washington, 230
Burger, Ralph, 132
Burns, H. S. M., 18, 93, 123, 193
Burns, John, 42, 102
Burroughs Corporation, 3, 150
Burton Mercy Hospital, 152 n.
business, as autocracy, 186-187; master's degree in, 93; society and, 92; as youngest of professions, 89; *see also* American business
Business Advisory Council, 199-201
business clubs, 159-171
business leader, change in public's

view of, 40; new responsibilities of, 223-225
businessman, challenge of to Communism, 236; stereotypes of, 89-90; as target in Washington, 189
business morality, 41, 225, 235

Cabot, Paul, 180
Cadillac division, General Motors Corporation, 49
capitalism, health of, questioned, 174-175; shaping of, by labor, 227
Carnegie, Andrew, 8, 161
Carnegie Institute, 168
Catholic Youth Organization, 150
Celanese Corporation of America, 102
Cerro de Pasco Corporation, 141
chairmanship, dividends on, 112-115
Chance Vought Aircraft, Inc., 135
charitable institutions, 155
charity drives, 146 ff.
Checchio, Mauro A., 219
Chevrolet division, General Motors Corporation, 48-50, 133
Chicago Club, 162
chief executives, shortage of, 177-178; *see also* director; executive(s); "top men"; presidency
Children's Home, Cincinnati, 149
China, trade with, 230
Christiana Corporation, 22
Chrysler Corporation, 41, 117-118, 126, 194
Church, Samuel Harden, 168
Citizens and Southern National Bank, 8-9, 120, 139
civil service employees, vs. businessmen, 190-191
Clark Equipment Company, 101, 127
Clay, Gen. Lucius D., 81, 162
Cleveland Welfare Federation, 149
club memberships, 59, 159-171
Colbert, L. L. ("Tex"), 42, 126, 133
Cole, Edward, 14, 49-51, 133, 226
Collyer, John L., 199, 234
Columbia Broadcasting System, 102, 116, 121, 132, 234
Columbia University Graduate School of Business, 173-179
Committee for International Progress in Management, 88

238

# INDEX

"committeeism," 47

Communism, challenge to, from American businessman, 236; struggle against, 222

community affairs, executive and, 111, 146-158

Community Chest, 147

Community Club, 212

Community Health Association, 152 n.

*Company Manners*, 59

competition, "dog-eat-dog" type, 232; intensity of, 125

Congress, U.S., as "outside directors," 190

Connor, John, 10, 46, 138, 144, 147, 173

Consolidated Edison Company of N.Y., Inc., 176

Container Corporation of America, 135

Continental Can Company, Inc., 81, 102, 181

Convair Division, General Dynamics Corporation, 195

Cordiner, Ralph, 24, 35, 45, 121, 126, 142-143, 176-177, 192, 227

Cornell University, 210

"corporate citizenship," 154-155

corporate giantism, 47, 52, 231

corporation, vs. community, as focal point, 211; nonpartisan politics of, 220; partisan political stand by, 210, 217

Corvair, "compact" car, 48, 52

"Coster, F. Donald," 183

cost-of-living clause, labor contracts, 228

*Country Gentleman*, 61

Cresap, Mark W., 90, 102

Cresap, McCormick & Paget, 102

Crowell-Collier Publishing Company, 62

Crown, Henry, 54

Cuban Air Products Company, 176

Cuban-American Sugar Company, 157

Cullman, Joseph, 137

Curtice, Harlow, 29, 50-51

Curtice, Leroy, 29

Dart, Justin, 15, 206

David, Donald K., 40, 91, 93, 176, 180, 183

Davis, Arthur Vining, 128

decentralization, 45-46

decision-making, 37, 42, 45, 122

Delaware & Hudson Railroad, 135

Democratic party, conservatism in, 217; Johnson & Johnson panel discussion and, 218

Denver *Post*, 54

Detroit, Mich., automotive center in, 48-52, 89

Detroit Council of Churches, 152 n.

Detroit Edison Company, 3

Detroit-Tomorrow Committee, 151

Detroit Urban League, 152 n.

Deupree, R. R., 199

director, *see* board member; *see also* board of directors

*Dr. Zhivago*, 135

Dodge, Joseph M., 190

dollar, stability of, 229

Donner, Frederic G., 3, 7, 36, 52, 114, 117, 126

Douglas, Donald, Jr., 23, 72-73

Douglas Aircraft Company, Inc., 23, 72

Downtown Lower Manhattan Association, 150

drinking, problem of, 124-125, 138

du Pont, Irénée, 22

du Pont de Nemours, E. I. Company, Inc., 13, 16, 22, 27, 45-47, 57, 85, 95, 112, 215, 220-221

Duquesne Club, 159-171, 235; membership and election to, 164, 170

Easter Seal campaign, 148

Ecker, Frederick H., 128

education, 61; aid to from American business, 233-234; problems of, 233-234

Educational TV Foundation of Detroit, 152 n.

Eisenhower, Dwight D., 162, 190-191

Empire State Building, 54

employee relations, 40

Engel, Clair, 219

engineer, as management executive, 86-87

entertaining, social and business, 132-133

entrepreneur, 40; age of, 39; incentives of, 44

Eppert, Ray R., 150-151

Erie Railroad, 205

Esso Standard Oil Company, 209;

*see also* Standard Oil Company of New Jersey
ethics, business, 225, 235
European businessman, vs. American, 224
European Common Market, 231
Evans, Thomas M., 98
executive(s), capacity for work in, 223-224; demands on, 112-129; development of, 93-94; home life, 130-145; increase of good manners in, 116; as "jack of all trades," 82-83; maldistribution of, 101; proper staff assistance for, 141-142; qualities required in, 34; recruitment of, 96-111; shortage of, 177; specialization of, 84-85
*Executive Suite*, 22
executive talent, circulation among, 100
executive wife, *see* wife, executive
experience, accumulation of, 31-32

Fairless, Benjamin, 169
Fair Trade laws, 232
Family and Children's Service, Minneapolis, 150
family backgrounds, 28; in recruiting of executives, 107
family control, through father-son succession, 66-79
"family man," 145, 244
family ownership, 36, 67-68
father-son succession, 66-79; *see also* boss's son
Federal Corrupt Practices Act, 213
Finkelstein, Rabbi Louis, 225
Finletter, Thomas K., 192
First National Bank of St. Louis, 29
Fisk University, 152 n., 154
Flagg, Gurdon, 163-165, 169, 171
Ford, Henry (founder), 3, 39, 77, 223
Ford, Henry II, 3, 77, 100, 162
Ford Foundation, 5, 40, 176, 183
Ford Motor Company, 3, 49, 67-68, 77, 99, 176, 180-181, 220
foreign businessmen, vs. American, 88-89
foreign cars, 49
"foreign giveaway," 230
foreign trade, 229-230
*Fortune*, 82, 98, 164
Fox, Harold, 219

Frank, Clint, 162
free enterprise, 203; responsibilities of, 232
Freeport Sulphur Company, 24, 138
free speech, labor politicking and, 212
Fund for the Republic, 220
fund raising, 146, 153, 158
Funston, G. Keith, 90, 137

Galvin, Robert, 16, 77-79, 135, 137, 156
Gateway Center, Pittsburgh, 157, 170
General American Oil Company, 55
General Dynamics Corporation, 17, 117, 137
General Electric Company, 16-17, 24, 34-35, 45, 58, 85, 99, 101, 118, 121, 142, 176, 181, 183, 185, 199, 220, 227-228
"general" executive, 82-83
General Mills, Inc., 2-8, 135
General Motors Corporation, 7, 14, 29, 36, 48-51, 74, 99, 101, 114, 126, 226, 228; attacks on size of, 231
General Petroleum Company, 121
generals, as corporation heads, 81-82
General Telephone & Electronics, Inc., 19, 32, 45, 119, 138, 144
General Tire and Rubber Company, 39
Georgia Power Company, 128, 148
Getty, George, 23, 134-135
giantism, corporate, 47, 52, 231
G.I. Bill of Rights, 57
Glidden Company, The, 13, 37, 117, 214-215
Goldman, Sachs and Company, 182
gold standard, 229
Goldwyn, Samuel, 37-38, 128, 141
Goodrich, B. F. Company, 181, 199, 234
Goodyear Tire & Rubber Company, The, 132
Gould, Jay, 205
government, as customer of corporation, 214-215; involvement of, in business, 231-232; legislative vs. executive branches of, 190; strange atmosphere of, 189
government appointments, 185-201

government relations, 40
government spending, 204
Grace, Eugene, 22
Grace, J. Peter, 28, 69-70, 139, 149
Grace, W. R. & Company, 28, 69, 138-139
Gray, Archie, 202-203, 216
Great Atlantic & Pacific Tea Company, 132, 180
Great Depression, 55, 60, 101
Greene, John, 149
Greenewalt, Crawford, 13, 22, 26, 34, 49, 89, 94-95, 112, 139, 205, 215, 220-221
Gross, Courtlandt, 29
Gross, Robert, 17-18, 29, 125, 127, 131-132, 216, 233 n.
*Growth and Development of Executives, The*, 106
Guffey, Joseph F., 168
Gulf Oil Company, 93, 159-160, 166, 202, 216

Hacker, Andrew, 210, 220
Hampton Institute, 152 n., 154
Hanley, Edward J., 90, 134, 160, 206
Harder, D. S., 100
Harlan, C. Allen, 152-153
Harlan, Ivabell, 152
Harlan Electric Company, 152
Harriman, Averell, 200, 204
Hart Schaffner & Marx, 5, 135-136
*Harvard Business Review*, 175, 183
Harvard Business School (Harvard School of Business Administration), 40, 89-92
Harvard Club, N.Y.C., 163
Harvard College, 4, 148
Harvey's Hardware Store, 85
Hatch Act, 213
Hazard, Leland, 26, 115, 117, 157, 167, 235
Heinz, H. J., Jr., 28, 75, 137-139, 166, 173
Heinz, H. J. & Company, 68
Hill, David, 136
Hilton, Conrad, 24-25, 127, 230
Hitler, Adolf, 168
Hoffman, Paul G., 200
Holden 25 automobile, 51-52
Holman, Eugene, 19, 116, 199
Hong Kong, world trading center, 230
Hood, Clifford, 160

Hope, Bob, 64
Hope, Stanley, 209
Horner, H. Mansfield, 118, 127, 134
Hotpoint Division, General Electric Company, 99
Hot Springs, Va., 199
Howell, Ward, 102-104, 107, 110
Hudson, The J. L. Company, 3
Hughes, Howard, 38
Hughes Aircraft Company, 38, 195
Hughes Tool Company, 38
Humphrey, George, 161, 200
Hunt, Roy, 166

Illinois Central Railroad, 18, 54
income, as incentive, 22-23
income taxes, take-home pay and, 22-25
individual, worth of, 227, 235-236
industrial relations, 216
Industrial Revolution, 186
inflation, dangers of, 228-229
inheritance tax, 57, 60
Inland Steel Company, 16, 68, 72, 76, 136, 187
Internal Revenue Service, 183
International Business Machines Corporation, 15, 28, 42, 76, 94, 121, 137
International Correspondence Schools, 57
International Institute, 152 n.
International Shoe Company, 68
Iron Curtain, 40
isolationism, remnants of, 229
Ivan Allen Company, 149

Jersey Standard, *see* Standard Oil Company of New Jersey
job hunting, 97-98
Johns-Manville Corporation, 220
Johnson, Frank, 96
Johnson, Robert Wood, 218
Johnson & Johnson, 218-220
Johnston, Eric, 200
Johnston, Wayne, 18, 54, 127, 148
Jones, James C., 51 n., 151
Jones, J. Hornsby III, 66-67
Jones & Laughlin Steel Corporation, The, 22, 137, 160, 166-167
Jonsson, Erik, 19, 121
Josephson, Matthew, 72
Joyce, Dwight P., 13-14, 37, 117, 119, 149, 214-215, 228
Judson, Frank, 169

Kahn, E. J., Jr., 182
Kaiser, Edgar, 74-75, 109, 118-126, 143, 214
Kaiser, Mrs. Edgar, 143
Kaiser, Henry J., 74-75
Kappel, Frederick, 16, 22, 30-31, 36
Kaye, Sammy, 81
Keiser, David, 157
Keller, K. T., 41, 118, 169, 194-197
Kellstadt, Charles H., 180
Kestnbaum, Meyer, 5, 136, 191, 203
Kimball, Dan A., 219
Kindelberger, J. H., 54
Knight, Goodwin, 219
Knight, John S., 162
Knowland, William F., 219
Knudsen, S. E., 74
Knudsen, William S., 74
Koenig, Robert P., 141
Koon Kreek Klub, 12
Koppers Company, Inc., 93, 159, 166
Korean War, 49, 182, 185-186
Kreuger, Ivar, 40
Kronenberger, Louis, 59

labor legislation, need for, 228
labor unions, acceptance of, by management, 227; elimination of merit system by, 226; pension and retirement benefits of, 128-129; political activities of, 212; political power of, 40, 186, 202, 204
Ladies' Home Journal, 61
Laidlaw, Walter, 153
Lambert, Chester, 219
Landon, Alf, 168
Lane, Mills B., 9, 120, 124, 139-140
League of Nations, 168
Lenin, Nicolai, 227
Leskoli, Joan, 91
Lever Brothers Company, 64, 117
Levis, J. P., 47, 83, 118-119, 142, 150, 155
Lewis, John L., 160
Lewis, Roy, 224
Life Extension Examiners, 18 n.
Lilly, David, 80
Links Club, N.Y., 162, 164
Litchfield, Edward Harold, 82
Little, Arthur D., Inc., 135

Little, Royal, 24, 118, 141
Litton Industries, 17, 21, 91, 119, 125
Lockheed Aircraft Corporation, 17-18, 30, 125, 127, 131-132, 216, 233 n.
Lowell, Abbott Lawrence, 89
Luckman, Charles, 64, 117

MacArthur, Gen. Douglas, 84-85
McCabe, Thomas B., 199
McCarthy, C. J., 135
McCarthy, Joseph R., 208
McClellan Committee, 208
McDonnell, James, 17, 26, 29, 39
McDonnell, William, 29
McDonnell Aircraft Corporation, 26, 39
McDonough, J. J., 148
Mace, Myles M., 91-92, 106
McElroy, Neil H., 162, 200
McGinnis, Patrick, 23, 139, 141
McGovern, John W., 207-208
McKesson & Robbins, Inc., 183
McKinsey & Company, 173
McNabb, Joseph, 62-63, 65
Macy, R. H. & Company, Inc., 176
Magee, Frank, 159-160, 167, 169
Malcolm, Wilbur, 37
Malik, Charles H., 236
management, art of, 81-90; board of directors as instrument of, 172 ff.; as profession, 81-84; shortage of executives in, 177; see also executive(s); middle management
Management Methods, 86
management recruiters, 101-102
management team concept, 42-43
management theory, 82-83
Marcus, Stanley, 5, 70, 142, 148
Maremont, Arnold H., 215
Matson Navigation Company, 133, 136
May, Louis F., Jr., 218
Meadows, Algur, 55
Mellon, Richard K., 93
Mellon, T. & Sons, 167
Merck & Company, Inc., 10, 46, 135, 138, 144, 147, 173
merit system, elimination of, by labor unions, 226
Merritt-Chapman & Scott Corporation, 134, 144
Metropolitan Club, 164

Metropolitan Life Insurance Company, 128
Metropolitan Museum of Art, 150
middle class, "new," 210
middle management, political parties and, 217
Michigan State University, 154
Mikoyan, Anastas I., 4, 19, 222
Mikoyan, Sergo, 222
military leaders, as corporate heads, 81-82
Milton Roy Pumps, 86
Minckler, R. L., 121-122
Minnesota Orchestral Association, 150
missiles, program, launching of, 194-196
Mitchell, Don, 32, 45
Mitchell, William E., 128
Moley, Raymond, 216
money, as incentive, 22-23
Monsanto Chemical Company, 139
Montgomery Ward & Company, 45, 136
morality, business, 41, 235
Moreell, Ben, 167, 169
Morgan Guaranty Bank, 83, 150
Morgens, Howard Joseph, 90, 149
Mortimer, Charles G., 173
Morton, Thruston, 217
Moses, Robert, 156
Motorola, Inc., 16, 77-79, 135, 137, 155-156
Munford, Walter F., 159
Munson, Charles S., 176, 181, 183
Murchison, Clint, 12-13
Murrow, Edward R., 208
Museum of Modern Art, 147
Musica, Philip, 183

N.A.M., *see* National Association of Manufacturers
Nance, James J., 99
National Association of Manufacturers, 16, 205-209, 220; public image of, 207; reasons for public dislike of, 208-209
National Bible Week, 150
National Biscuit Company, 102
National Cash Register Company, 32-33, 98-99, 150
National Dairy Products Corporation, 181
National Distillers Products Corporation, 176

National Gypsum Company, 43, 127, 204
National Industrial Conference Board, 180
National Press Club, 112
nepotism, 74; *see also* boss's son; family ownership; father-son succession
New Deal, 198, 204-207
New York Central System, 73, 101
*New Yorker, The*, 182, 184
New York Philharmonic Symphony Society, 18, 157
New York Stock Exchange, 90, 137, 183
*New York Times*, 168
*Newsweek*, 51 n., 151, 153
Nickerson, Albert, 28, 109, 137, 191
Nieman-Marcus, 70
Nike-Ajax missile, 197
Nixon, Richard M., 204
Nixon-Rockefeller struggle, 1960, 204
nonpartisanship, political, 216-217
North American Aviation, Inc., 54
Northwest Airlines, Inc., 74, 123, 230
Nyrop, Donald, 74, 123, 230

Ohio Bell Telephone Company, 149
oil industry, 12-13; 55-56; boards of directors in, 179
Olds, Irving S., 234
O'Neil, Thomas, 38-39
Opinion Research Corporation, 207 n.
Ormandy, Eugene, 34
Owens-Corning Fiberglas Corporation, 180, 199
Owens-Illinois Glass Company, Inc., 47, 83, 118, 142, 150
owner-management, 41

Pace, Frank, 19, 117, 137, 162
Pacific Gas & Electric Company, 34, 43, 127
Pacific Union Club, 163
Packard, *see* Studebaker-Packard Corporation
Paepcke, Walter, 135, 162
Paley, William S., 116, 121, 132, 139, 146-147, 234
Pan American World Airways, Inc., 234

# INDEX

Pardue, Austin, 167
Pasternak, Boris, 167
Patterson, J. H., 33
Paxton, Robert, x, 17, 34, 58, 118, 228
Penney, James Cash, 25, 30, 54-55
Penney, J. C., Company, 25
Pennsylvania Railroad, 168
Pentagon, Washington, D.C., 195-196
Pepsodent Division, Lever Brothers Company, 64
Percy, Charles H., 16, 60-65, 77, 113, 137, 187, 215
personnel, developing of, 93-94
Philip Morris, Inc., 137
Piedmont Driving Club, Atlanta, 120
Pillsbury, Philip, 150
Pillsbury Mills, Inc., 68, 73
Pittsburgh, Pa., cultural leadership in, 158
Pittsburgh Coke & Chemical Company, 166
Pittsburgh Plate Glass Company, 26, 115, 117, 136, 166, 169
political candidates, corporate contributions to, 213
political education, nonpartisan program of, 216-218, 221
politics, business and, 202-221
Ponzi, Charles, 40
Porgy and Bess, 37
Porter, H. K., Company, 98
Potter, Stephen, 47
Power, Donald, 19, 119, 138, 144
Presbyterian Hospital, N.Y., 150
presidency, of company, 64; demands on, 112-116
Price, Gwilym, 167
price cutting, 232
Procter & Gamble, 90, 149, 199
Proctor, David, 166
productivity, labor's wage demands and, 228
professionalism, disrespect for, 158; doctrine of, 81-82; glorification of, 175
profit motive, 21-22, 235
profits, distribution of, 187
profit-sharing plans, 44
Prudential Insurance Company of America, The, 38
"psychological minute," 115
publicity handouts, 209, 216-217
public relations, 6, 17, 27, 40, 47-48, 81, 114, 188; community activities and, 148, 152-153, 216; "corporate citizenship" and, 155
Public Utility Holding Company Act, 207

Queeny, Edgar, 139

Racquet Club, Philadelphia, 164
Radio Corporation of America, 42, 53, 102
Railway Express Company, 54
Ramo, Dr. Simon, 11, 83-84
Ramo-Wooldridge Corporation (Thompson Ramo Wooldridge, Inc.), 11, 83
Rand, Henry H., 68
Randall, Clarence, 136, 187, 191, 193, 198
Rathbone, M. J., 94, 109, 173
recession of 1957-58, 189
recruiting firms, 102-106
Red Feather campaigns, 146
Reed, Philip D., 16, 126, 200, 229, 234
regulatory legislation, N.A.M. opposition to, 206-207
Republican businessmen, 217; schism among, 203-204
Republican party, predominance of, in big business, 203
Republic Steel Corporation, 227
retirement benefits, 128-129
retirement plans, 125-126
Reuther, Walter, 135, 162, 168, 227
Reutherism, 228
Rexall Drug Company, 15, 206
Reynolds, R. S., 98
Reynolds Metals Company, 98
Rich, Richard H., 70, 120, 136
Rich's, Inc., Atlanta, 70
Richardson, Sid, 12
Riesman, David, 210
risks, business, 43
RKO Pictures Corporation, 39
"robber barons," 26, 222
Robber Barons, The, 72
Rockefeller, John D., 133
Rockefeller, Nelson, 162, 204
Rockwell, Col. Willard F., 98, 230
Rockwell Manufacturing Company, 98, 230
Rolling Rock country club, 162
Romney, George, 7

Roosevelt, Franklin Delano, 201, 230
Roosevelt Administration, N.A.M. and, 206
Roper, Daniel C., 199
Row, Edgar, 117

salaries, executives', 223
Sammons, Wheeler, Jr., 27
Sarnoff, Gen. David, 42, 53, 102
*Saturday Evening Post*, 52, 61
science, exploiting of, 83-84
Schmidhauser, Harold B., 115
scholarship programs, 153-154, 158
Scott Paper Company, 199
Sea Island, Georgia, 199
Sears, Roebuck & Company, 180
Securities Exchange Act, 207
security, vs. *élan vital*, 226; premium on, 99
self-confidence, 224
self-criticism, 234-235
self-education, 61
self-employment, 226
service industries, growth of, 210
Sevier, Randolph, 133, 136
Shanks, Carrol M., 38
Shell Oil Company, 18, 93, 123, 193
Sinatra, Frank, 81
Sinclair Refining Company, 120
Sligh, Charles R., Jr., 208
small businessman, N.A.M. and, 209
small cars, 48-49, 51
Smith, C. R., 123, 138
Smith, E. Everett, 173, 175
Smith, George Albert, 92
Smith-Corona Marchant, Inc., 82
Snyder, John W., 200
Snyder, W. Cordes, Jr., 118, 204
socialism, 202, 204; state vs. corporate, 15
Social Security benefits, 128, 206
Socony Mobil Oil Company, Inc., 28, 109, 137, 191
Somervell, Gen. Brehon, 82
Sonnenberg, Benjamin, 6
Sorenson, Charles, 77
South America, executive shift to, 59-60
Southern Company, The, 31, 43, 47, 124, 130-131
Soviet Union, "competition" with, 4; value of individual in, 235; *see also* Communism

Spatta, George, 101, 127
specialists, need for, 84-85
Spencer, P. C., 120
Sperry Rand Corporation, 82
Spiegel, Fred, 139
Standard Oil Company of New Jersey, 5, 19, 94, 116, 179, 199
State Street Investment Corporation, 180
Stevens, Raymond, 135
Stevens, Robert T., 200
steel industry, 8, 18; executive "circulation" in, 100
Stewart, Rosemary, 224
stockholder relations, 40, 48
stockholders, democratic process and, 172-184; formality of approvals by, 172-174; partisan politics and, 215, 220-221
stock options, 22-23, 44, 96, 103, 105
Studebaker-Packard Corporation, 99
success, dedication to, 19, 225; theory of, 29
Swope, Gerard, 199
Sylvania Electric Products, Inc., 32; *see also* General Telephone & Electronics, Inc.
Symonds, H. Gardiner, 90

Taft, Robert A., 5, 135
Taft-Eisenhower split, 1952, 203-204
tariff, protective, 229-230
taxes, income, *see* income taxes; *see also* inheritance taxes
"team," vs. one-man operation, 42-43
Teamsters Union, racketeering in, 228
Tennessee Gas Transmission Company, 90
Texas Instruments Incorporated, 19, 121
Texas oilmen, 55; *see also* oil industry
Textron, Inc., 24, 118, 141
Thomas, E. J., 132
Thornton, Charles B., 17, 21, 119, 125
time-saving, approaches to, 115-116
"top men," actual job functions of, 120-129; self-confidence of, 224; self-criticism among, 234; short-

age of, 177; *see also* chairman; executive(s); presidency
Tracerlab, Inc., 19, 116
Trans World Airlines, Inc., 38
travel, business, 118-119
Trippe, Juan, 234
Trotsky, Leon, 227
Trudeau Sanitarium, N.Y., 85
Truman, Harry S., 124, 185, 194, 219
trust-busting, 231
Turen, Inc., 92
*Twentieth Century Capitalist Revolution, The*, 154, 235

*Uncommon Man, The*, 89
Union Carbide Corporation, 220
Union Club, N.Y., 163-164
unionism, acceptance of, by management, 227
Union League Club, 5, 163
United Aircraft Corporation, 118, 127, 134
United Community Funds and Councils of America, 150-151
United Foundation of Metropolitan Detroit, 151-153
United Fruit Company, 4-5
United Service Organizations, 152
United States Chamber of Commerce, 16, 29, 209-210, 220
United States Rubber Company, 207
United States Steel Corporation, 18, 133, 159-160, 164, 166, 169, 234
University Club, 164
University of Michigan, 82, 154
University of Pittsburgh, 82
University of Toledo, 150
U.S. Industrial Chemicals Division of National Distillers Products Corporation, 176

vacations, forced, 141-142; how spent, 142-143; number of, 140-143
Vanderbilt, Commodore Cornelius, 36, 39, 72-73
Vanderbilt, William, 72-73
Vanderbilt University, 150

Wabash Railroad, 31
wage demands, vs. productivity, 228

*Wall Street Journal*, 38
Wallace, Henry A., 135
Ward Howell Associates, 102 ff.
War Manpower Commission, 191
War Production Board, 192
Warner, W. Lloyd, 56
Washington, D.C., effectiveness of businessman in, 189, 193; fear of, by young executives, 191-192; government appointments in, 185-201; "healthy exposure" to, 198-199; time required for "breaking in," 192-193
Watson, Thomas, Jr., 15, 28-29, 43-44, 76, 94, 121, 137, 142, 147
Watson, Thomas, Sr., 42, 44 n.
Wayne University, 154
Webb & Knapp, Inc., 38
Weinberg, Sidney James, 181-185, 199-200, 234
Westinghouse Electric Company, 90, 102, 167
White, Charles M., 227
White, William, 135
Whiteford, William K., 160
Whitney, Eli, 140
Whitney, John Hay, 200
*Who's Who in America*, 27, 161
wife, executive, 107-110, 130-131; child-raising responsibilities of, 144; understanding required in, 143-144
Williams, Langbourne, 24, 138
Wilson, Charles Edward (General Electric), 185-186, 194, 200
Wilson, Charles Erwin (General Motors), 185, 188-189, 192, 200, 228
Wilson, I. W., 169
Wolfson, Louis, 134, 144
Wooldridge, Dr. Dean, 11, 83
work week, executive's, 115
World War II, 49, 57, 77, 182, 198-199, 223, 229
World War III, 186

Yale Alumni Board, 150
Yale Club, N.Y.C., 163
Y.M.C.A., 148, 152 n.
Yondetega Club, Detroit, 162
Young Presidents' Organization, 114

Zeckendorf, William, 38
Zenith Radio Corporation, 99